This book is dedicated to Stu, Neil, Archie and family, Nigel, Blakey, Ben, Rhys, Matthew and Terry, Colin and everyone at the Westgate. Thanks also to Dai (also of the Westgate), Carl, Dave O'Gorman, Jock and all the characters I've met along the way. Thanks to Paul B, Richard B, Paul V and Paul. Thanks to Vince Alm and Tony Jeffries. Thanks for support from Annis Abraham and Carl Curtis. Thanks to everyone who has made me laugh on the message boards. Thanks to Tony Rivers and Meic Gough. Thanks Jon Candy for photos for the blog and the cover of this book. Thanks to Terry Phillips (I honestly think the *Echo's* football coverage is much better than a lot of people make out). Thanks for support from my mum, dad and family. Thanks of course to Cardiff City FC. And thanks most of all to AC x

The Blues are Back in Town

A year and a lifetime supporting Cardiff City

Nick Fisk

PARTHIAN

Parthian, Cardigan SA43 1ED
www.parthianbooks.com
First published in 2015

ISBN 9781910409824
Cover design by Rob Harries
Typeset by Elaine Sharples
Printed and bound by Gomer Press, Llandysul, Wales
Published with the financial support of the Welsh Books Council
British Library Cataloguing in Publication Data
A cataloguing record for this book is available from the British Library.

The Blues are Back in Town

Contents

He wasn't to know it, of course, but my dad made one fairly crucial error when I was growing up. The first football match he took me to was between Swansea and Spurs. Could he not have realised that my fate must involve me becoming a Cardiff City fan, and how potentially painful this early memory might prove to be?

But I've always thought you choose your own path in life. You can't let things from your childhood affect the way you live your life as an adult too much, I don't think. You can't be forever harking back to your school days or blaming other people for the way you turn out later in life. You have to take control and do the right thing, and that's why doing the right thing for me was always about getting down to Ninian Park and being amongst fellow fans of the Bluebirds.

These days, it's the Cardiff City Stadium, and for too long we had to endure the bizarre experience of watching our team play in the wrong colour. The 2014/15 season was the one where finally this changed and things were put right. If the season was memorable for no other thing, it would be that. The subject of the rebrand was by far the biggest talking point amongst Cardiff fans, and indeed, the world media in fact, for the whole time it was in place. Now that the whole sorry saga has come to an end, hopefully we can concentrate on seeing some decent football again; let's hope new life is breathed into the stadium now that the bitterness has passed.

This book documents the season with the match reports I wrote as part of a blog I kept called The Fisk Report. I've tried to make them a bit more interesting than regular match reports – there are some accounts that barely mention what happened on the pitch at all. This may be more to do with the fact that I've got a poor memory or didn't make enough notes. But football is always about more than just the football.

Perhaps that's the part that people who don't follow football never quite get. Maybe the third section of the book might give any non-football fans who happen to pick this book up a bit more understanding of what else goes along with being a fan.

And just for good measure, I've put in my account of the fight to have our colours restored – ultimately, thank God, a successful mission. The day Cardiff City went back to blue, a large tree blew over right outside my house. It certainly seemed as if this was the wind of change passing through.

Section 1:

Season 2014/15 – August-December

'The thing about football – the important thing about football – is that it is not just about football.'

TERRY PRATCHETT

August/September 2014

There was hardly a feeling of optimism at the start of this Championship season. Cardiff had survived just the solitary season in the Premier League, we were still being managed by Ole Gunnar Solskjaer, who did not seem to have any clear plan for the team, and a poor start to the season meant that before the end of September, he would be given his marching orders.

In addition, there were still not too many players in the squad that fans could be enthusiastic about in terms of delivering the goods for the forthcoming season, regardless of who was in charge. Coupled with that, we were still playing in red; Swansea were still in the league above us... there were many reasons why it was a testing time to be a Cardiff City fan.

From a personal perspective, my interest had definitely begun to fade. It wasn't just the drop from the Premier, but the match day experience, for me, was just not what it once was; sitting in a silent stadium is not the way I prefer to watch football. However, I was to be given a good reason to make an attempt at rejuvenating my interest in Cardiff City when a publisher, who I had submitted some writing to about my time as a fan (see Section 3), gave me a contract to keep a blog over the season. It was an offer I could hardly refuse – getting paid to write about the football team I support – and so of course, I jumped at the chance. But that was not to say that any negative feelings simply disappeared; I was a fan like anyone else, and so was engulfed in the same gloom that loomed over us all.

August 13
Coventry City 1-2 Cardiff City: Why are the Bluebirds playing Coventry City in Northampton in red?

This game could be looked at as typifying what some people might refer to as the downside of modern football, which usually is a metaphor for how money talks. A team known as the Bluebirds, but who were now playing in red due to the whim of a rich owner, met Coventry City, who due to the fact that they couldn't afford the exorbitant rent charged to play at their own ground, were having to play at their temporary home of Northampton, thirty-five miles away. For Cardiff, it could be said it was a case of one man having too much money and power, while at Coventry there was not enough of either, although it would take a diligent Coventry fan to properly explain the ins and outs of their own situation. In each case, the upshot was protests from fans in an attempt to force change.

Along with this, however, is another new aspect to the game – and that is fans of opposing sides feeling the need to jointly express their mutual pissed-offness. I found myself at this game as me and the g/f, Christina, were in Coventry anyway for the Goliath poker tournament, being played ironically enough at the Grosvenor Casino attached to the Ricoh Arena, Coventry's official football ground!

After a visit to Christina's gran who lives in Northampton (her permanent home, she hasn't been made to live there, although to make matters more confusing, she would have preferred to still be living in her original home of Bournemouth), we made it to the Sixfields Stadium a few minutes after kick-off. We'd bought tickets, and in fact found that the turnstiles were now closed, and we had to bang on the gates to be allowed in. You get that sort of thing at smaller grounds, I guess.

Well, we took our places amongst a good away following for a first-round Capital One Cup game that was also being televised. My first instinct was to turn to the Coventry fans, in their guise as the home supporters, and jeer, 'Is that all you take away?' Obviously, this is a common chant to fans of the away team who might have travelled some distance, but I thought it could work equally well directed at the meagre 'home' support, who in this instance had had to travel thirty-five miles.

I can't say there was much of an uptake for this chant. Maybe it's because I've never been the best at garnering support for one of my own chants, but more likely it was because I'd missed the point, unaware that it had been decided in advance that Cardiff fans at this game were here to show support for the opposition's own misfortune.

So had I taken the wrong approach? There's no doubt that Cardiff's support has changed in recent years. The hooligan aspect seems almost a thing of the past, with fans now being much more family-friendly. But should that mean adopting a watered-down attitude in general? Surely an aversion to fans of the adversary is part and parcel? Let's face it, if it had been Swansea who'd been made to move to, say, Port Talbot, the jokes would have come thick and fast – they have hardly held back on taking the mick out of our own situation vis-à-vis Tan and the evil red. Coventry is a side that really we have no bones with, but are they a side that, on the flipside, we should automatically show a collective brotherly love for? On a personal note, it was at Coventry that two friends were arrested back in the days when police treated arresting Cardiff fans like a national sport.

The amusing thing about Coventry's temporary home was that it was itself in the process of being reconstructed! Builders working on the stand being rebuilt had downed their tools for the evening to watch the game. Other non-paying punters were a group of around twenty or thirty Coventry fans on a hill outside the ground who held up banners of protest, clearly feeling that refusing to pay the £10 entry fee was an effective way of voicing their objection to the situation, while at the same time, they could save themselves money and still get to see the game.

Cardiff's early goal, which had been scored before we'd got in, ensured that the Bluebirds were mostly in pretty good voice – and yes, as expected, almost the entire Cardiff crowd were in blue (another irony as, in the past, Cardiff fans rarely wore colours at away games, with a good number instead preferring smart designer clothes, but anything blue is de rigueur now). A lull on around thirty minutes gave me the opportunity to start another chant I'd dreamed up. 'Can you hear Northampton sing?' I shouted at the Coventry fans, and again, I failed to get support for this one.

But then something happened that I hadn't quite expected. I mean, I'd seen it coming, because the paper signs I'd seen on the floor had said it would happen, but on thirty-five minutes, most people on both sides held up these paper signs which had 'Let Down' written on them, and this was the staged moment at which both sets of fans could express their combined dissatisfaction. Further songs were sung, and the game itself even stopped as the players took a drinks break.

For me, these sort of staged events are atmosphere killers. Perhaps that's the idea. But I'm really not sure if it's right for both sets of opposing fans to be doing this as a unified effort. I even sensed that some Coventry fans weren't that sure about it, because despite some Cardiff fans urging them to 'Stand up if you feel let down!', some of them looked to be doing this with some reluctance, I felt, due to uncertainty as to whether they should do this at Cardiff's requisition.

So then the game got underway again. Oh yes, the game! Cardiff continued as the better side, and sustained pressure resulted in another goal late in the second half (albeit, an own goal). Coventry quickly pulled one back for a slightly tense finish, although it always seemed fairly certain that Cardiff, much the dominant side, would hang on for the win.

The whole nature of the protest meant that attention was drawn away from the match itself and, like I say, had a detrimental effect on the overall atmosphere. It worked if that was the intention, but it did seem a little sad that people had travelled some distance to be part of a night of negativity.

One more traditional aspect of Cardiff's away support, particularly at these smaller grounds, was maintained, and that was the constant ribbing of the home team's goalkeeper. Poor old Burge, in the Coventry goal, came in for a constant barrage of stick from the Cardiff fans. He was told, after about the twentieth time of asking, that if he did the ayatollah, we would leave him alone, but he stuck to his guns and refused the invitation, even after a Cardiff player had shown him what this gesture entailed. In fairness to him, I think he was actually a pretty good keeper – never really thoroughly tested, but he dealt with everything effectively.

So a victory was achieved, and we sang, as you do, about being on our way to Wembley. Some things just don't change.

This was Christina's first ever Cardiff City match. Sadly, as both our mobiles were playing up, we didn't even get a picture of her at the game, but she's got her ticket as a memento. It was not a classic, but she'd learned a few things about what it was like supporting Cardiff, as things are now, and also as they always have been. When it was 2-1, there was even the old chant of being 'the best behaved supporters in the land (but a right bunch of bastards when we lose)'. Just who this bastardry would have been directed at if we'd lost though was not quite clear – surely not our newest friends, the Northampton-based Coventry fans, who we'd spent most of the rest of the match being sympathetic towards?

The good news for Coventry was that within a week of this very game, the announcement was made that, like naughty children who had spent time at a friend's until things calmed down, they could now return to their lovely Ricoh Arena home. Cardiff fans had at one point chanted, 'Stand up for your history', which definitely did not sound right as Coventry only began playing at the Ricoh ten years ago.

As for Cardiff, who knew what fate was in store for us? Unlike Coventry's mid-season switch, unless the FA took an exceptionally lenient view, I didn't imagine going back to blue would be a mid-season option for the Bluebirds. But the whole situation of the team playing in one colour, and fans wearing another, really was starting to look a bit ridiculous – would Tan ever see sense?

September 13
Cardiff 2-4 Norwich:
Norwich versus Fisk Family Wedding

I missed the Cardiff v Norwich game, and a good thing too, by all accounts. To throw away a halftime lead of 2-0, and end up losing 4-2 reeks of haplessness of the highest order, despite the fact that Norwich were a team with some good current form, and of good pedigree. My reason for absence – is a wedding a good excuse? And it just so happened to be a Fisk wedding, where I learned for the first time that my grandfather, hailing from Norfolk, was in fact a lifelong Norwich City fan. Just why my dad had neglected to ever before impart this knowledge upon me, I'm not quite sure. None of my grandad's three sons kept up support for the Canaries, so old man Fisk can't have been too persuasive of the merits of following the East Anglian side.

Norwich's is a ground I've still yet to visit. It's always seemed a bit of a long way, although I have been to nearby Ipswich, so perhaps it's not just the distance that's kept me from going there. Maybe it's because it's not a team that has ever filled me with too much enthusiasm. Yellow has always seemed to me to be a bit of a suspect colour for a home strip for a start (Brazil, perhaps, being the exception). Red I can understand, though not for Cardiff, naturally. I suppose yellow is a primary colour, so you wonder why it's not taken up by more clubs. There's no yellow corner in a boxing ring of course. With it being the colour of custard, you might think it has cowardly connotations, which is hardly the spirit for a sporting team. Could it be considered as the Lib Dem option of colours, neither one nor the other? And not just custard, it's also, of course, the same colour as mustard, and if there's one thing Norfolk is famous for, it's mustard.

These are the things you find yourself writing about when you miss a game. It's like with anything, if you've not been to a place, all you have are the most common clichés about it. I'll be referring to its residents as each having just four fingers next! And don't mention Alan Partridge! Certainly not in the presence of The Kabeedies, a favourite band (though sadly they are no more) once a part of the Norwich music scene (and each with all fingers intact, as far as I recall, when I last interviewed them), although actually, the football enthusiast of the band, Rory, was in fact a Watford fan, so erm, not quite sure why The Kabeedies are getting a mention here.

In recent years, Norwich's celebrity owner, Delia Smith, caused the biggest stir (no custard/cookery pun intended) with her cringeworthy rabble-rousing plea to inspire passion in fans, and the immortal words: 'Let's be 'aving you!' It was one of those situations where everyone basically knew what she was trying to say, but also immediately realised that it sounded distinctly wrong. It'd be like a policeman saying to a football fan as he's being arrested, 'I'm taking you on an away trip', or something along those lines.

The main thing that makes me cringe about Norwich City is, to me, they've always seemed to epitomise the notion of a family-friendly football club. They travel in large numbers, all in their brightly coloured replica shirts, and it all appears like jolly good fun, but at the same time, just a little staid. This kind of support might be the sort of thing people who run football clubs might prefer these days – it's not problematic and it's easily maintainable. It's the sort of thing the owners of Cardiff seem hell-bent on trying to transpose on Cardiff fans. But is it really fun? Fun's not something you can force. Or not something you can fake anyway. Maybe I'm wrong, but I just question whether wholesome family fun really is fun. I'm sure there are many Norwich fans who'll argue that I've got it all wrong. But having just got back from a family wedding – all very nice, no complaints at all – I can vouch for the fact that family events can be, well, just a little boring. If what Delia craved was a bit more excitement from the fans, maybe what she really needs to do is start up the Kick

Families out of Football Campaign! And maybe, just maybe, that's why my grandad preferred to go it alone when supporting Norwich, and not get all his sons involved...

September 16
Cardiff 1-0 Middlesbrough: Missing: Soul – If Found Please Return to the Cardiff City Stadium!

I'd arranged to get a ticket for this game from Annis Abraham who'd posted on facebook that he had a spare ticket going. Annis is one of Cardiff's most notorious fans, known more recently for his books on the club, his popular online message board, and for leading fans in protest against the club hierarchy (his previous reputation is of course a little different).

We'd arranged to meet at what is now Maverick's, though will probably be known forever to most Cardiff fans as the Ninian Park pub. There was a bit of a cock-up, however, as I had waited inside, while Annis had been waiting outside, and for some reason, neither of us had thought to check where the other was! So I'm not sure what Annis did with the ticket in the end – I know he attended the match himself – but I ended up getting a walk-up ticket from the ground.

One of the battles Annis won, along with others, was convincing the majority of fans not to support the rebrand. I sometimes wondered if Annis was still smarting over the fact that he was not more instrumental in trying to resolve the issue prior to the start of the 2012 season, which subsequently meant a long drawn out remonstration instead. Once again, by far the majority of the crowd for this match were in blue. But it seemed like they were all feeling blue as well. As if it wasn't enough to be watching a team of players that no-one knew too well, that had just been relegated, being managed by someone who didn't seem to really know what he was doing. It's not really ideal to be sitting in a soulless stadium if people are not going to pipe up in support of a team that's quickly gone behind.

The silence throughout was extraordinary – excruciating even. Whereas Cardiff fans at Ninian Park would sing relentlessly, at the new ground the habit of staying silent has pretty much stuck. I do feel sometimes it almost seems out of laziness. I'm not quite sure what it is, but it's a sorry state of affairs that herd mentality has led to a collective state of reticence, the crowd like zombies waiting to be risen from their slumbers. And it was no use forever pointing the finger at Tan (who no longer comes to watch now that Cardiff are no longer in the Premier League) – the atmosphere was bad even before his arrival at the club.

The point about this stadium is that if you just want to come and watch a football match, it's a good place to do it – the view from just about anywhere is good. But isn't there more to watching football than just watching football? If you just wanted to watch a football match, you might as well just go down to a park and watch a kick about down there. Isn't it more to do with being a part of a lively crowd, getting caught in the moment?

What made things even worse was that this was a particularly bad example of a football match. With just three shots on target between the two teams all game (just one from Cardiff), there was little in the way of goalmouth action, and very little action across the entire pitch. A bit like watching paint dry, would be one way of putting it, and if there's one thing more boring than watching paint dry, it's watching paint dry in a soulless stadium filled with 19,000 people who are doing nothing much but watch the paint dry with you, occasionally shouting out that the paint isn't good enough.

'Paint dry! It's just like watching paint dry!' If someone had just got this chant started it might have cheered people up, the chant echoing the more familiar 'Brazil! It's just like watching Brazil!' when a team is playing well, though I can't see that one being used too much any longer, unless it's used ironically when a team is facing a 7-1 defeat.

I don't think I'd ever found myself actually hoping that the away team might get a second goal so I could justify leaving the godforsaken place early. As it was, I hung around to the end, in the vain hope that Cardiff would do the thing that hadn't looked likely for the entire duration and score a goal. Towards the end, the Canton Stand even did a fake goal celebration (one of the few times the 'singing section' of the stadium bothered to make any noise at all), so desperate had we become. If there's no action forthcoming, the next best thing is to pretend was the thinking, I suppose.

But on the message board, there was apparent denial of the silence of the painfully silent crowd. 'Our fans were fantastic tonight,' Annis himself said in one post. 'The Canton Stand sang and cheered the team on many occasions.' Aside from the fact that there's the admission (by omission) that the rest of the crowd was silent, it's incorrect that even this designated singing section made much in the way of noise. It really was one of the most dismal experiences of my life, and I couldn't see how things were going to improve – brushing the problem under the carpet was not going to help!

But I don't think it was just fans who were to blame; the team, the stadium, what was going on at the club, or any of that. In the time I had to reflect on life in general, it occurred to me that maybe this is just the way things are going – maybe the tradition of football as a live spectacle is dying out? It can be more fun to watch in the comfort of a pub, pint in hand, the option of nipping out for a fag whenever you like (at the Cardiff City Stadium, they don't even let you go for a cigarette until the designated time, i.e. during the half-time break). People seem more enthralled by things happening online than on the pitch – there is probably more excitement generated on Annis's message board than at the game itself – all the talk on the message board before and after the match can be more interesting than the match!

Everyone has suddenly become an expert on football. I swear that, back in the day, we couldn't really give a monkey's about formation, the team needing more width, any of that nonsense. It was more about meeting up, having a pint and a laugh, coming up with a few stupid chants, singing along to all the regular songs, from the back of the stand, where you could barely see the game anyway with a hulking great post obscuring the view! And I usually missed the goals, going for a piss cos I'd drunk too much!

September 20
Cardiff 2-2 Derby: Old Boys Give Cause for Cheer

Derby County gives me the opportunity to visit another Fisk – my older brother lives in nearby Etwall. Arriving the night before the match, I was treated to a takeaway curry, which in true Fisk wallet-watching tradition, we collected – despite the shop being around five miles away – for the ten per cent discount! I have to say, it was the poshest takeaway shop I've ever seen, with leather seats and a flat-screen TV in the waiting area, and even the day's paper, rather than a leftover from the previous week. A fine beef madras meant I went to bed with a nicely warmed stomach in preparation for match day.

The day started well for me. I arrived at Pride Park intending to buy a ticket from the ground. Although around 1,500 advance tickets had been sold to Cardiff fans, there were still some available on the day. I went to the away turnstiles to ask where to buy one, and a steward pointed me in the right direction, but then called me back and very kindly handed me a spare one for free! Something like this had never happened to me before, and I felt extremely lucky – it definitely made up for the slight ticket mishap at the previous game. I thanked the steward, and walked in. Paying four pounds for a pint inside definitely did not seem so bad!

This was the first game following the departure of Ole Gunnar Solskjaer, who left the club with an estimated £1 million pay-off. However many nice things people have said about the man, this seems an extraordinary sum of money for someone who had been in a job for not more than eight months and was an extraordinary failure.

But ring in the new... or the not so new. Solskjaer's makeshift replacement came in the form of a double-headed beast, namely two favourite Cardiff City old boys: Scott Young and Danny Gabbidon. Mainstays of the team from yesteryear, Scott Young secured legendary status with his winning goal against Leeds Utd; Gabbidon was always solid and reliable, good enough for a regular place in the Welsh squad when, under Mark Hughes, and during Sam Hammam's reign at Cardiff City, Wales could draw a crowd to fill the Millennium Stadium. Those were the days, as Mary Hopkin might say, and the familiar old songs for the former Cardiff favourites were sung loud and proud.

Cardiff fans were in great voice for this one (oh, if only this could be replicated at home), in stark contrast to Tuesday night, when Solskjaer was last in charge, though sadly, in the first half, the football was still a little pedestrian. The team seemed to start brightly enough, but then Derby took control. They had a goal disallowed for offside, and it took a couple of great stops from Marshall to prevent them going ahead. I think I was probably in favour of the Scots reclaiming their own land in the referendum two days before, but if it had meant for any reason, perhaps due to needing a visa of some kind, Marshall not being allowed to play for Cardiff City, perhaps it was fortunate for us that a No vote was declared.

Just like the Coventry game, the first half again featured some rounds of applause at set points in the match – three in total at this one, with a joint clap for Brian Clough on ten minutes, a Cardiff chanting session at around 19:27 into the match, and then more mutually approved applause on twenty-two minutes for a Derby fan who was recently murdered.

You start to wonder if it won't be long before every minute of the match will herald some reason or other for remembrance, and again, I do feel it detracts from the spontaneity of more customary methods of showing support.

Mind you, as a guy next to me suggested, there was little to cheer about on the pitch, so it wasn't such a bad thing to practice applauding. This was the same man who had moved seats because of excessive body odour, he told me, and if there's one thing to make you sweat, it's someone telling you he's moved to stand next to you because of it!

Our on-pitch performance improved dramatically in the second half. Half-time had been spent outside where talk of our next potential permanent manager was on many fans' lips. The names of Pulis, Lennon and others were bandied about –

perhaps Gabbs and Young could even stay on, I suggested, in a similar way that the once temporary manager for another Welsh club had done?

It certainly seemed like their combined half-time team talk may have worked, with Cardiff coming out much stronger following the break. Gunnarsson's goal on fifty-one minutes sent Cardiff fans wild, but with the knowledge that one goal was unlikely to be enough to win the match. A second goal from Whitts four minutes later sent Cardiff fans into a near state of delirium with the thought that a two-goal lead with thirty-five minutes remaining was likely enough to seal victory. For a good few minutes Cardiff were in control, and I have to say, as fans once again raised the noise levels up high, I was starting to think that this was one of the best away games I could remember, and it really did feel like the good old days.

Sadly, the lead was short-lived. Derby pulled one back on 61 minutes and now hanging onto a lead again seemed a difficult prospect. In recent years, Cardiff's method of play in these situations has been to sit back and hope to defend from their own half, instead of continuing to play a more natural game. Attacking teams seem to always pick up on this. The situation was probably not helped when I jinxed things by muttering to the man next to me that we really did not want this one to be a draw; inevitably, moments later, Bryson was powering in a drive from outside the box which even Marshall could only stand and watch.

It was disappointing. A draw away from home is usually considered a reasonable result, but not in these circumstances, i.e. when we were two goals up, seemingly cruising, and against a side that we possibly did not deserve to beat, and also, of course, as we were now in the bottom half of the table, and really needed to be seizing opportunities for points. '2-0 and you fucked it up' jeered the Derby fans, and it sadly did ring true. Both sets of fans really added to the entertainment value of the day, in fairness.

I left as soon as the whistle went to go and receive a call from Bill at Cardiff Radio, who was asking for a quick update. Otherwise I would definitely have preferred to stay and applaud the team, who I did feel put in a good performance. It was only the lack of resilience towards the end that let them down. Not too sure if either of the substitutions helped – Le Fondre on for Noone, and Maynard on for Gunnarsson, but Noone was probably not considered fit for a full ninety minute outing.

Cardiff's inability to hold out for the win obviously tainted the occasion, but overall, with two senior former stars taking charge instead of an ex-Man Utd player, there seemed good reason for optimism. It had been a slow burner, but it felt as if the season was beginning to start, even without it being fully set alight. I couldn't get my lighter to work straight away for a younger fan outside, but then it did, and I was on my way. Even without the win, today felt like a good day to be a Bluebird.

September 23
Cardiff 0-3 Bournemouth:
Young Fans Make Old(er) Fan Smile!

Cardiff lost 3-0. That's pretty much all I've got to say about the game itself. I'd hoped Christina might make it to this one, being from Bournemouth, but unfortunately, she'd started a job in Bristol and couldn't make it.

I once again found myself in Maverick's, aka The Nin, prior to the match. A little on the empty side, but not as quiet as The Westgate, where I'd first put my nose into. This didn't bode well for the night's attendance, which after all was not expected to shatter records, being only a Capital One Cup game, and not a glamour tie exactly (at this stage in the season, nobody would have expected it would be Bournemouth who would be crowned champions of the league).

I did see old chums from The Westgate, Terry and Matthew, in The Nin. They told me how they were planning to make a weekend of it for the Blackpool game next week, and in fact were planning to stay for three nights! I was told by a friend of theirs who was going to be the driver for the trip, that it was 'good because you can have three days of drinking, and then a day off when you're driving back.' Now, forgive me if my logic is askew here, but I couldn't quite make sense of this sentence. Surely it would have worked just the same if it had been one night's stay and thus 'good because you can have a night of drinking, and then a day off when you're driving back', or on the flipside, if a month's stay was planned, this also would be 'good because you can have a month of drinking, and then a day off when you're driving back.' I did wonder if he had already used this justification for the three-nighter, and had gotten away with it, perhaps due to the other person, most likely his other half, not quite concentrating on what he was saying.

Terry and Matthew, a little ahead of me in their finishing of drinks, went ahead to the match, so I stayed and talked with the staff of The Nin. They told me the extremely sad news that the pub was in fact going to close, after Brains pulled the plug on the place with a mere two weeks' notice.

I think most people will agree that the pub has already lost a little of its character since being changed from the Ninian Park pub to Maverick's. You'd have to ask the staff why this decision was taken a couple of years back. But the essential aspect of the place – it being the last place Cardiff fans can stop before going to the match (from the Canton direction), and then of course, the first place to stop coming out from the match – had remained intact. And along with that, always incredibly friendly staff – this feature was the same for the whole time I've drunk there, i.e. many, many years (obviously not one session).

Just take for example last week – they had run out of Stella on tap, so I was served two bottles of Stella for the same price as a pint. Now, the logic in this, you might think, was just straightforward, but so many bar staff would not even think of doing something like that.

The Ninian Park pub was the place that so often we would be downing either a pint or a spirit minutes before kick-off, safe in the knowledge that, as we always said, 'They never kick off without us!' It would be the place to return to at the end of the match, as all the results were coming in.

It could be quite a rowdy place, but in the main, everybody was always friendly as, after all, we were all Cardiff fans! It was a great place for celebration, especially after a big win. Or more recently, after the last home game at Ninian Park, there was the comedy moment when someone walked in with a door that had been taken from the ground, which was in the process of being dismantled! This door was then signed by everyone who was in the pub that day – I seem to remember there was even quite a famous former player who signed it (was it Jason Perry?).

There was a guy I used to remember seeing in there – this

is going back some time now, maybe as much as twenty years – who would sit at the bar, and remain there for the entire duration of the game. As my memory serves, he would not go to the game itself, because he truly considered himself to be so much of a jinx that he'd rather just sit in the pub till after the game was over! Or maybe it wasn't that, maybe he didn't go due to a player being sold. Something like that. I remember quite admiring him for taking a stand anyway. Similar to people who've taken a stand and won't go because of the rebrand. In fact, for one match only, I did a similar thing, and went to The Nin on the first day of the 2009 season – Cardiff's first proper game at the new stadium – refusing to go to the match after the disastrous end to the previous season dished up by Dave Jones, including losing our last ever game at Ninian Park, 3-0.

It was outside The Nin that I saw Burberry being worn for the first time. It may have been worn by fans for some time, but I'd never really paid attention to it. I just saw a couple of fans wearing it – this strange brown check, had no idea what brand it was – and then noticed that it was becoming increasingly popular, so that before long, it was a staple part of many Cardiff fans' fashion sense, before becoming absurdly widespread across the whole country. I'm pretty sure that Cardiff fans were among the first to start this trend, especially as the factory that made the stuff was based in the Valleys. When this factory closed Cardiff fans began to no longer wear it.

The Nin was definitely a place for the more fashionably dressed fans back in the day – I used to see people wearing things like Tommy Hilfiger, Ralph Lauren, all that kind of stuff. All those labels were beyond my price range, but I did buy some quite smart stuff from a shop once, including a striped Full Circle jumper, some nice baggy jeans and a 3/4 length raincoat which, one time, I wore in The Nin. I had this bizarre experience of someone coming up to me and saying in a low voice, 'Us hooligans should stick together!' Pretty sure he was actually being serious, but it did sound quite funny.

I was in The Nin the time the police actually surrounded the place so that we couldn't leave – completely insane situation. The whole issue with trouble between police and fans at just about every match had got to a bit of a peak, and I think this was the police's way of saying they'd had enough. It was a bit strange though because away fans were rarely seen in and around The Nin, so the exact intention of the police was uncertain.

Just so many memories of the place. Billy the Badge would come in, and you always had that moment of just not knowing quite what to say – you really had got quite enough badges, but then again, Billy was always so friendly and he quite often would have a new badge that looked tempting. I saw Billy at this particular game in fact, at half-time when the score was 3-0 (as it would remain). I asked him if he had any 'We're shit and we know we are' badges. He said he had the match-day badge, 'If you want a memento?'

At half-time, so many Cardiff fans really felt that they could not endure much more – some might even have been tempted to leave. I thought I might as well stick it out. I decided, if I'm going to do this I might as well go to the back where there were a few fans who might possibly get a few chants going. Once again, for me, it was not just the sorry state of affairs on the pitch, but the quite sad spectacle of fans doing very little in the way of getting behind the team. With a much more sparse crowd than usual, and of course, after seeing three goals scored against us, there were definitely mitigating circumstances, but come on – at least the Scott Young chant when it was announced he was leading the team for the first time at home? There was not even a roar (which is usually followed these days quickly by hush) when Ali made the announcement encouraging us to 'make some noooise!' Tonight, this was instead followed by a hush, followed by further hush.

So as I say, I went up to the back where, at the beginning of the second half, a few fans were making a bit of an effort to try and enjoy themselves by singing. A couple of familiar chants, then a chant of '4-3, we're gonna win 4-3', and from then on the tone was set – we were going to enjoy ourselves regardless of what else happened.

These were mostly quite young fans – average age of around twenty. They started to sing, 'Come join us' to other nearby fans on our side, and before long, there were a couple of hundred at the back – now we had enough to be heard. The Bournemouth fans were not going to heckle us for being quiet this half! Songs old and new came out, and it was sustained, almost non-stop, with barely a break between songs, for the whole of the second half. It goes to show that everybody does know all the songs, it's just that so often the songs aren't getting properly aired.

There were even some quite entertaining songs made up on the spur of the moment, such as one for Danny Gabbidon who'd picked himself to be part of the team. When someone else of about my age sat down for a moment, the chant went up, 'Do you need to have a rest?' That one really made me laugh, and should be used more often for seated fans, I think.

I think when we did the Poznan, followed soon after by the Conga, it really felt like a minor miracle was occurring – Cardiff fans actually enjoying themselves at the Cardiff City

Stadium. I remember very little about what happened on the pitch in the second half. I know that Bournemouth did not score any goals, so it did feel as if our vocal support was helping a little in that respect – there was one goalmouth scramble when I think four attempted shots were blocked. What these young fans were doing was simply not sticking to the script. All we were ever hearing about was the familiar Cardiff City story, which people had become obsessed about, letting it grind them down. Why shouldn't people still just enjoy themselves while supporting the club they love – they're not going to simply stop supporting the club while times aren't so great after all, so why not try to enjoy yourself even during those hard times – it's like people dancing when a war's on! Who cares?!

Of course, the circumstances at this particular fixture helped. With it being a cheaper ticket, many younger fans could afford to come, and these were the ones making all the noise, putting many older fans to shame. Also, as the Canton stand was closed, there was no option but to allow a "singing section" nearer to the away fans – you really do think that the club should consider reorganising the layout of the stadium to allow this. But even so, this "minor miracle" almost didn't happen at all – we were more familiarly quiet for all of the first half. It just took a few people to get it going in the second half, and show that this could easily be done for all home league fixtures, when there are far more people there, so far more who could help make a lot more noise!

Well, gripe over. It's going to get tiring if I keep going on about this issue. Despite a heavy defeat, I walked away for the first time feeling quite light-headed – I was actually happy! I was walking away from the CCS feeling happy. And I think there were many others like me, not just those who'd joined in with the chants, but others who had not had to simply sit and wallow in the misery of what was presented to us on the pitch. So I'd like to say thanks to a smallish band of young fans for making an old(er) fan smile.

I walked back past Maverick's, now a little sad again at the thought of it closing. A light rain had started, reminding me that I had better get the windscreen wipers on the car fixed soon.

September 27
Cardiff 2-1 Sheffield Wednesday: Morrison-and-on-and-on

There are two Morrisons in Cardiff. Actually, that's not true – there's the one down the Bay, the one in Llanishen, and the more recently opened store on Newport Road (excellent meat selection, and even better value if you have money-off vouchers) – which makes three Morrisons. With the addition of loan signing Ravel Morrison, there were now two Morrisons playing for Cardiff City, but instead of offering a range of quality meats, the hope was that these new additions to the squad would be providing passes and goalscoring opportunities.

I thought I heard the Canton Stand singing, 'One Morrison, there's only one Morrison!' which I thought might actually work as an entertaining chant. This was shortly after Ravel Morrison came on for Noone, making a total of two on-pitch Morrisons. It may in fact have been the more regular chant for Scott Young however. And unfortunately, if it wasn't the Canton Stand singing 'the Morrison chant', now that I've suggested it, it will of course, never be sung, because as everyone knows, new chants never start online or in print. Someone could dream up the greatest chant of all time, but as soon as it's written down, it won't get heard on the terraces (at grounds that still have terraces), because the only songs that get heard on the terraces are those started on the terraces.

Ravel Morrison (who wore his first name on the back of his shirt, either to avoid or add to confusion) was nothing short of a revelation. He's a player who has courted controversy. You get these maverick players – incredible football talents who go off the rails. As a player, you could see straight away that here was someone who was a master of his trade, with a lovely touch and balance, and good awareness of those around him. His only flaw that I could see, in the half hour that he was on for, was not trying out a shot a couple of times, but other than that, he looked like a player who could transform the Cardiff side completely – could he sustain his output over 90 minutes though, or was he only effective as a super-sub? We would have to see.

There were times, particularly in the first half, when I did start to question how some of Cardiff's players could justify their five-figure weekly wages. If you pay a plumber to come to your house, surely you wouldn't expect him to start dismantling your bathroom, so why should I, as a paying punter, have to watch a footballer being paid vast sums of cash deliver crosses that gently drift into the penalty box and drop safely into the arms of the opposition's goalie? I'm not going to name names, but no-one should have too much difficulty in realising who I'm referring to.

I was just about to finally join the crossed-arms, moaning-with-grim-expression brigade, commenting that Whitts might as well just pass the ball along the turf for all the success he was having with a more conventionally floated free kick approach when, finally, he delivered a beauty, which Morrison (Sean) connected with perfectly, heading the ball into the back of the net, and sending fans, who may not have expected the lead, into the first stages of rapture.

It was another game where Cardiff's opener was against the run of play, so it again seemed a precarious lead. This proved the case when Morrison undid his own good work with an own goal just after the start of the second half, and the scores were once again level.

The Sheffield Wednesday side that came to the Cardiff City Stadium were on reasonable form (the 7-0 midweek Cup defeat to Man City aside), and captained by Glenn Loovens. The former Cardiff defender was once a part of a very strong backline that also included the formidable Roger Johnson. It was a combination comparable in strength to the other noteworthy Cardiff defensive duo of Gabbidon and Collins. It would be nice if a new Cardiff defensive partnership could be formed – perhaps when Turner returned he would partner Manga? The Gabonese international looked strong and solid, leading attacks from the back.

After the own goal, pleasingly for a change, Cardiff dug deep and really began to play some quite attractive football. They even looked like a team with a bit of purpose and determination. The passing started to come together far more effectively, and they began to create a few more chances. It suddenly looked like quite a strong team out there, making Sheffield Wednesday look fairly poor. It wasn't likely that either team was going to be in the mix for promotion, but if Cardiff could keep up the level of commitment shown in the second half of this match, there was still hope.

Gritty persistence and a really excellent bit of skill from

Pilkington on sixty minutes meant that Cardiff were ahead once more. Yet again, for the last few minutes, we were hanging on just a little, and the injury time free kicks Wednesday were granted didn't aid in calming nerves, but it was not nearly as nervy a finish as it has been for some other City matches.

There was no clear area where Cardiff showed dominance – not in defence, midfield, or up front – but collectively, as a team, there were more promising signs, and with one or two good individual performances as well, such as Manga's, as mentioned. It was looking as if Marshall as captain might even work – certainly, our most experienced player had earned the right to wear the skipper's armband and 'marshall' matters.

Just who would be called on to permanently manage off-field matters remained unclear. Russell Slade was the bookies' massive odds-on favourite at 1/10, and it seemed most likely given that he had actually now resigned from his Leyton Orient post. However, if results continued, keeping Scott Young remained an option, I felt – in interviews, he spoke like someone who would like to give it a shot. The prospect of Tony Pulis now looked forsaken.

This additional cause of anxiety at the club meant that fans were still not in particularly good spirits – a return to the league, with the legions of season ticket holders, meant there was no impromptu partying as had been during the Cup game against Bournemouth. Handball shouts from both Wednesday and City fans (neither given) ensured a bit of banter. The Sheffield support mocked our claim to always be blue, but you wonder how they would feel if they underwent a rebranding – would they put up with a name change, say, if a wealthy owner preferred the sound of Sheffield Sunday?

The party at the Ninian Park pub (Maverick's) didn't quite happen as planned, from what I saw anyway. There were a good number of people there before the game (mostly outside), but with absolutely nothing left on tap, only bottles and cans were being sold, so there would have been very little left to party with. Nonetheless, a good attempt was no doubt still made at completely drinking the place dry.

October/November

So, the new manager was brought in: Russell Slade from Leyton Orient, as expected. He had hardly been the No.1 choice of fans (most might have preferred Tony Pulis) – surely recruiting a manager formerly of a none too successful lower league club was a gamble at best? But he had to be given a chance was the feeling, and results, at home at least, were good to begin with, even if there were not scintillating displays of attacking football. Hardly the stuff to get worked up about, and the muted atmosphere at the stadium remained. Practically the only chant fans would get behind was one of protest: 'We'll always be blue' was sung loudest, and with blue scarves all around the stadium while the team played in red, the situation was starting to get ridiculous. At least when Wales came to play their home Euro fixtures at the Cardiff City Stadium there was more reason to be cheerful. 'We're the Welsh international side, we'll always be red' might have been heard, ironically.

October 10/13
Wales 2-1 Bosnia and Cyprus: Double the Dragon

It's said that there's nothing certain in life except death and taxes. In my own experience, the two certainties are: picking up speeding fines, and that there will be at least one Wales international football match on or around my birthday. This year my birthday fell on a Sunday and was sandwiched between two games; Wales were due to face Bosnia on Friday and Cyprus on the Monday. It is a bit of a double-edged sword for me. It's nice that there's always a match to look forward to, but I sometimes wish that I had other things to look forward to on my birthday other than another Wales match.

For my younger brother, the Bosnia game was going to be a little more special. He is friends with the husband of one of the Welsh FA's main ticketing managers. Gary, the husband, is more of a rugby fan, so often declines his wife's offer of complimentary tickets to Wales games, but on this occasion, he couldn't refuse as she was able to offer two hospitality tickets, including meal, etc. which included sitting at the same table as James Dean Bradfield of the Manics! So despite it being close to my birthday, it was my brother getting the VIP treatment, though he's hardly an ardent Wales fan himself (he's one of those people who prefers to watch England if Wales and England clash on TV), but I didn't mind taking my place in the 'cheap seats', amongst the rest of the regular supporters.

Before the match, I'd hoped to meet up with old mucker, Dave O' Gorman (aka D.O.G.), who could hardly be at a more polar extreme in terms of support for the Welsh football team than my brother and his mate. I first met Dave on a Wales away trip to Austria around ten years ago. Due to lack of funds I've only been to four Wales away games (and only two overseas), but I can vouch for the fact that international away trips are among the best experiences you can have in terms of being a football fan. For one thing you get to meet people like Dave. With an extraordinary capacity for beer, and an all-round good bloke, Dave travels to just about every Wales game, including from Germany, where he now lives, back to Wales, for the home games. He is also the captain of the Wales Supporters Team.

Let me introduce you to the concept of the Wales Supporters Team. According to their website – www.walessupporters.co.uk – the idea was conceived in an Armenian bar in 2001, and the very first game they played was against Finland in 2002. Basically, fans of Wales meet up with fans of the team Wales are due to play and, well, have a game of football. Simple, you might think, but brilliant at the same time. A glance at past results makes interesting reading – a 13-4 defeat to Russia ST in 2010 must have been an entertaining spectacle; a 6-1 away win against England ST must have been one to savour.

I watched the Wales Supporters Team versus the Scotland Supporters Team on a bitterly cold day in Glasgow in March 2013. Despite the cold – there was even some snow – I had a warm feeling inside with the knowledge that here was a very good thing indeed. Being a supporter of the Wales Supporters Team is in my view just about the best thing in the world. I might even fancy having a game for them – just about anyone who turns up at a game with a pair of boots will at least be given the chance to come on as a sub – but I'm still not sure if that would beat being a supporter of the team. Wales STFC lost that game against Scotland STFC 5-1, but still, the effort couldn't be faulted, and I know for a fact that a good attempt was made to beat Scotland in the drinking stakes in a pub near to Hampden Park prior to the Scotland v Wales game proper.

Unfortunately, this time, I didn't meet Dave after all – I knew he'd be at The Full Moon in town, where a pre-match party was planned, but I didn't make it there until much later in the day, by which time he must have moved on. The place was still crammed with Wales fans though – I suspect the owners might have connections with the Welsh language scene – they used to have a good collection of Welsh-language record sleeves on the walls around the place, which included one of my favourite singles of all time – the 'Colossus' EP by Crumblowers.

There were also no Wales Supporters Team games to watch this time as they're normally only scheduled for the away games. So instead, I went along to the Wales v Bosnia match with my good pal Harry, who as it happens I also met for the first time at that Austria v Wales game. We had seats in the new section at the CCS, which had been quite empty in Cardiff's first season back in the Championship, but an impressive crowd of over 30,000 filled the stadium. The Friday night atmosphere was electric and it's a great view from this new upper tier. I didn't even mind too much being in the red seats, given that it was a Wales game, although we actually managed to sit in some of the white seats which form the 'decorative' aspect of the seating.

One of the focuses of the current campaign has been the slogan 'Spirit of '58', as 1958 was the last (and only) time Wales qualified for a major tournament. It only occurred to me while watching this game why this should be the focus; if we manage to qualify for Euro 2016, it will of course be fifty-eight years since 1958! The group Wales had drawn suggested we were in with the best chance for a long time, and being led by Gareth Bale, who could be compared in ability and stature to the late great gentle giant, John Charles, it certainly would be a fitting time for us to qualify again. With the clock on 19:58, Gunter missed a left-footed shot which would have been perfect.

It was an exciting game, full of energy, without ever quite reaching boiling point, aided by an ebullient crowd of Poznaning Bosnians and vociferous Welshmen. Wales were effective in defence, and needed to be, in the first half especially; Hennessey confirmed his status as Wales' No.1 with some great saves. In the second half, Wales were more attacking; Williams perhaps should have put one away, and then in injury time, Bale delivered a lightning bolt long-range shot that was well stopped. I felt for much of the match that whoever took the lead would win the game, but instead, the game stayed goalless, which was good enough for Wales to stay top of the group ahead of the Cyprus game which we could definitely hope to win.

Spirits were high as we headed for the exit, though this task in itself was tricky for those in the packed upper tier. The drab, narrow stairwell here has the look of a high security prison – all grey brick and metal – and would do nothing to ease the pain following a heavy defeat: stadium bosses would have been wise to take note and brighten it up before future Cardiff City matches.

Another factor for officials to look into was the lack of alcohol. It seems completely bizarre that fans should be forced to endure a two-hour prohibition. Throughout both games banners for Brains Brewery were displayed in the advertising hoardings, yet despite the fact that Brains beer is apparently available at this very location, no beer was being served to the thousands of potential customers. Why should this be?

Do Brains really believe that football fans are a bunch of puritans who will shun the opportunity to buy their wares? Coke and coffee is available – is there a rumour going around that all football fans are caffeine addicts? The sight of thousands of men shuffling around at half-time, not sure whether to pay £2.80 for a bottle of Fanta to satisfy thirst buds was one to behold. At rugby matches, you can buy beer, and even take it to your seat. This really was an eye opener. And a potential conspiracy theorist's dream, as it was Brains – sponsors of the Welsh rugby team – who closed down the Ninian Park pub just a week before – essential for all beer-drinking City fans (who would have thought?). On the other hand, maybe they're just not legally allowed to serve alcohol.

From Bosnia we ventured to entertain Cyprus, one of international football's minnows, with a population of less than a million. Not quite such a big crowd for this Monday-night game, but still respectably above 20k. Wales took an early lead through Cotterill in the thirteenth minute, who deserved his (slightly fortunate-looking) goal, given that he should have scored moments earlier if he'd just elected to shoot instead of passing to Bale who was not positioned to score himself. Bale flicked on a beautiful ball to Robson-Kanu ten minutes later who carried on to finish sublimely, and Wales were cruising. We were now talking about a potential avalanche of goals and the opportunity to strengthen our goal difference, but that was not to be. Cyprus pulled one back with a goal similar in fashion to Cotterill's – a harmless-looking ball in that missed everyone, and somehow ended up in the back of the net – and then, early in the second half, King was sent off. It looked like a harsh dismissal, but no matter, this decision by the ref killed off the game as a spectacle. Even against ten, Cyprus never really threatened to draw level, but it made things harder for Wales, who equally made fewer efforts to march on to further glory.

Fans were definitely happy with a victory however – not very often will you hear Welsh fans singing about being top of the league. Perhaps it did not mean too much at this stage – we'd had two 'easy' games against Andorra and Cyprus, and it would be Belgium away next – but without doubt, things were looking positive. It seemed to be a group in which, as they say, anyone can beat anyone – Bosnia after all, lost at home to Cyprus – but as long as Wales remained competitive, we were hopeful of being one of the two teams that qualified automatically, with one more automatic place being granted than in previous tournaments.

Bale was not as much on fire in either game as he was against Andorra, and anyone betting on him to score would have been disappointed at his drawing a double blank. The massive expectancy placed on his shoulders can't have helped, although pressure has never looked like something that's worried him before. Being man-marked in the Bosnia match no doubt made things more difficult. Despite this, there are still times when he seems to command play to such a great extent that he looks like a father showing his kids how it's done; his speed, power and agility is still second to none. This is not to belittle any performances from other Wales players – Jonny Williams looked strong against Bosnia, but was curiously left out against Cyprus. It seemed especially odd given that Coleman complained of eleven players missing from the preferred starting line-up. It may have been that a slight injury meant he was an unused sub for this game; George Williams, who substituted him in the first match, was instead given a full try-out versus Cyprus. Ledley looked composed as ever in both games. Robson-Kanu's confidence also looked increasingly assured.

Vincent Tan may have wanted to see a red team of fire and passion playing at the Cardiff City Stadium, in which case all he needs do is sit in at a Wales international match.

October 18
Cardiff 2-1 Nottingham Forest: Time to Take a Stand

You get these every now and then. A result that pops up that is genuinely a surprise. The Championship leaders were in town, with an unbeaten streak stretching back to the start of the season. Perhaps the early kick-off hindered the Forest players, but theirs was a woeful performance, hardly befitting league leaders. There were a ridiculous number of passes completed straight to the touch line, practically nothing in terms of attacking power, and they even had to resort to trying to kick their way out of trouble (this failed), and were lucky to only pick up three yellow cards.

Cardiff did not need to be at their best to beat this under-performing side. Few mistakes and fairly routine football ensured the win. Being 2-0 up at half-time brought back memories of the defeat to Norwich earlier in the season, when the same half-time score line ended up in a 2-4 defeat. I overheard someone say that he'd been in Prague at the time of the Norwich game, had seen the scoreline at 2-0, had checked the time, and thought the game had finished. He'd neglected to take into account the hour time difference, so was naturally pretty shocked when he later saw the correct full time score!

Even Forest's fans were a little lacklustre. They began noisily enough, but quickly quietened down once Whittingham had doubled Cardiff's lead. I went to Forest, I think, 3 seasons ago, and I remember then thinking that they had a superb home support – it was the first time I think I'd ever felt that a home team had completely out-sung Cardiff's away fans, and therefore the first time that I realised that Cardiff's support – be it home, or even away, was starting to lack its usual sting. So it did come as a bit of a surprise that Forest's away fans were not quite so loud, even though they were behind – perhaps, like the players, they still needed an extra cup of coffee or two to wake them up properly.

There was the usual red/blue banter – and this was another one where, even in the third season since the rebrand, things did look a little odd. With Forest's home kit being red, now when they came to Cardiff, they had to play in their away strip (in this case, white). In the past, obviously Forest would never have had to have a change of strip when playing against Cardiff. It could be confusing, even more so if the second strip of a team that commonly plays in red is blue!

I had begun this game in a seat in the Ninian Stand, which was in typically sombre mood, in contrast to the lively atmosphere just days before for the Wales games. I had been standing, amongst others, but when a steward instructed us all to sit down, as they regularly do, I moved to the fairly empty section to my left, where I thought it would be ok for me to stand. A few minutes later, he came by again, asking people to sit down. If there had been someone directly behind me, and he had asked me to sit down, I would not have had any problem, but as I was not blocking anyone's view, I really didn't see that it would be an issue for me to remain standing. I told the steward that I preferred to stand.

He then quite angrily pointed to the designated standing section in the Canton Stand and said, if I wanted to stand, that's where I needed to go. If this really was the only option I decided that's what I'd do. I walked down the stairwell, around the foyer, and took a place in the Canton Stand instead.

Just for once, I felt like taking a stand, as it were. For far too long Cardiff fans had to endure excessively heavy-handed treatment from the police. Now we're expected to tolerate Gestapo-like treatment from our own stewards. It really is out of order. If I had not moved, what was this steward going to do? Throw me out? For standing up at a football match?! It's crazy! Supposedly, this is happening so that the club stays in line with the FA's policy on 'safe standing'. Just the other week, when I'd joined a friend in the very back row of a block, I was still instructed to sit down. There was supposed to be someone from the FA monitoring the situation at Cardiff. I really cannot imagine that he would have been able to return a damning report on how things are at Cardiff: fans at the CCS are in fact remarkably compliant; there must be many more clubs where 'persistent standing' (the phrase itself is laughable when you think about it) goes on far more. And besides, I really do not think that the FA actually wants to clamp down hard on fans anyway – I'm sure that, in their wisdom, they would much prefer fans to enjoy themselves, rather than feel constantly pressurised by jobsworth stewards. So therefore, it seems to me that, in their constant attempts to get people to sit down, the stewards are doing something that they don't even have the authority to be doing.

So anyway, in the Canton Stand, at least here, in the central section, everyone stands, because they're allowed to. People seem more relaxed, including the stewards. When this section is quiet though, in some ways, it's even more odd. Yes, the occasional chant is sung, though not especially loudly. As usual, God knows what it would have been like if we didn't have a two-goal lead. But when it's quiet, it's actually a bit disconcerting. It feels a bit like being amongst a crowd of lifeless robotic clones who are just waiting for the appropriate time to make an appropriate response.

After all, what difference does it make if the Canton Stand does make a noise? It's rarely enough to really lift the team, and the stand is too far away from the away fans for them to even be able to hear properly. It's like cheering at a cinema: what's the point if the people you would want to hear can't hear you? Or another thing it reminds me of is the Stephen Fry sketch where two old fools are sat opposite each other at an extremely long table, and are so far apart that every time either of them shouts something the other always mishears it. 'You'll always be scabs' is shouted at the away fans (as is the custom, in reference to Nottingham workers crossing picket lines during the miners' strike). 'We'll always eat cabbage??' they might well have asked. It's blatantly obvious that the Canton Stand should be switched to where the Family Stand (next to the away fans) is, but I'm not sure if this will ever happen.

Well, anyway, here was I moaning even when we'd won a game. It really was an incredibly easy win this one – Cardiff, as mentioned, really did not need to be too exceptional. Yes, we had the trademark slightly nervy finish after Forest pulled one back towards the end, with the trademark gesture by the players of parking themselves inside our own penalty box. The ref came to our rescue, though, by blowing the final whistle for once slightly prematurely. It really felt like everything was conspiring to help us out today; you might almost have imagined this one was fixed for Russell Slade's first game in charge.

So what of the new manager? In some ways, I reflected that a good standard lower-league manager could be better for us than a manager who had dropped down from the Premier League. At least he might be keen and eager to demonstrate his worth instead of being bitter. I wondered if Slade might be a bit of a yes man; he immediately complied after calls for him to do the ayatollah, but of course, there's no cause for complaint there. He had announced his intention to get the side fit and if he wanted to shake up the side a bit, that was also fine by me. Maybe it was time the team demonstrated their willingness to stand up and be counted; maybe then they might get to feel the noize.

November 8
Birmingham 0-0 Cardiff: A Little Injector Fluid Needed

You know that being a football fan is an addiction when you look at upcoming fixtures, see that there's not another game for a couple of weeks (and you're not even certain you'll be able to make that one), and realise that you've got no choice – there's an away game today which you weren't necessarily planning to go to, you know you can just about afford it, your mates can't go due to work/watching the rugby (lame)/other reasons, but sod it, you're gonna have to make it up there.

I was up bright and early on Saturday morning. I hadn't yet got a ticket, but I knew the ticket office was selling them right up until 12am (Birmingham's ground being only around a two hour drive, after all). If I'd been quick I'd have made it onto one of the Supporter's coaches, but I was still umming and erring. Finally, at around 10.30, I made my decision (I was going to have to drive now), and with the girlfriend still enjoying a Saturday morning lie-in, I hopped in the shower, got dressed, and was at the ticket office by around 11.30.

I must have been one of the last people, if not the last person, to buy a ticket. But it did occur to me that if there was anyone else still yet to get a ticket, they'd be driving too, and so perhaps it might be worth us sharing a lift. As chance would have it, a guy and his young son walked in, picking up tickets they'd booked over the phone earlier that morning. I offered £20 – about half of the estimated fuel cost for the return journey – and they were a little uncertain, but eventually, they went for it, and we were off.

In a similar way, it had been a last-minute decision for Kevin and his son, Nat, who were from Barry. Nat had been due to play football, but the game had been called off, so they made a quick change of plan, and had decided they were going to the match. I soon discovered that, barring a trip to Wembley, this was to be Nat's first regular away trip (pretty understandable, I think, that Wembley in some ways didn't count). With this in mind, I could fully appreciate that Kevin might have liked to share this experience with his son without the added baggage of a stranger.

Fortunately, we got on fine, making small talk for much of the way, and I hope that as we got closer to Birmingham they might no longer have considered me to be a total stranger. I made a slight faux pas at one point while we were discussing which parts of Wales were able to pool Cardiff fans from when I compared Barry to Neath. What I meant was that with Barry being close to Cardiff geographically, it's a stronghold in the same way that Neath is for Swansea fans, but immediately as I said this, I realised that potentially it could be considered a little insulting. I think Kevin and Nat were able to forgive this unintentional error. We stopped off at a services at one point, and as the traffic was so slow moving to rejoin the motorway, I got out to have a cigarette. As the traffic quickened, Kevin began to drive off, but fortunately, he was not intending to leave me behind.

We made it to St Andrew's with about a half hour to spare and were lucky to find a park close by. On our short walk to the ground we chatted briefly with an older Birmingham fan. I asked about their last win but he didn't seem in too optimistic a mood – I'd actually forgotten that it was only two games previously that they'd suffered an 8-0 home defeat to Bournemouth! Birmingham are another club with all kinds of off the field problems, sadly, and another club with an owner (who's now left) that caused financial problems. While ours at least has money, Birmingham were still playing in blue at home.

St Andrew's was a stadium that, despite its close proximity to Cardiff, I had yet to visit, so it was good to be able to tick another ground off the list. Possibly not quite as big a ground as I expected, it's a cross between an older and newer type of ground, not too big, not too small – just about right in many respects. A disappointingly large number of empty seats were visible though – clearly the home fans were a bit disheartened (they were also exceptionally quiet), and it definitely seemed like they were not enjoying their second-tier status, especially, no doubt, as long as Aston Villa and West Brom remained in the Premier.

Both teams went into the game with a strong desire for a win for different reasons. Birmingham wanted a win to maintain a bit of momentum after their last victory and to lift themselves out of the bottom three. Cardiff were in search of their first away of the season. A win here would cast off that gremlin as well as keep open hopes of promotion. I anticipated a gritty battle, not a classic game of football, ending most likely in a draw, and you know what? Fisk called that one, as that's exactly what we got.

This game heralded the return of Turner, which was good to see – a really excellent defender in my view – he makes the phrase taking candy from a baby his own when it comes to crucial tackles. It was a solid enough return, with many sensible trademark hoofs forward or out of play to ease any nervous situations at the back.

For Birmingham, Cotterill had to endure being frequently lambasted by away fans none too pleased that he'd at one stage elected to play for Swansea. Our fans were in good spirits, though I was surprised that, despite talk on the message boards, Slade songs were not emanating from the stands in honour of our new manager – surely as we got closer to Christmas, 'Merry Xmas Everybody' or a version of it would have to be sung?

Cardiff had the edge in the first half, and should really have scored at least one of the two one-on-one opportunities that were presented to first Le Fondre, and then Macheda. I was thinking at this point in the season that, potentially, this could be a good front line – Le Fondre was someone that I'd heard many fans say they were expecting more of, even if he was yet to fully deliver (he was to go on to complete a season of unfulfilled promise in a Cardiff shirt).

The second half, Birmingham were allowed back into the game. On sixty-three minutes, Wes Thomas had a goal disallowed, but this at least had the effect of rousing the Birmingham fans from out of the slumbers. Truly, until that point, it was as if many of them had forgotten they were at a live football match, and instead imagined they were listening at home on the radio with their feet up and a cup of cocoa.

As the game wore on, it looked increasingly likely that neither team was going to score, and this was how things panned out. Birmingham never had much to offer and frankly,

Cardiff should have been disappointed not to have made more of this chance to grab away points. Cardiff were now on a run of four away games without a goal – I imagined Cardiff fans, in desperation, having to copy FC Magdeburg fans who, following a string of results without scoring, stood in the stand behind the goal with giant luminous arrows directed towards the net as an aid to their strikers. And while I took the point of a guy next to me that Cardiff were not looking good away from home, I'm not sure he needed to spend around another ten minutes explaining the situation to me, and how he himself would do a much better job than Russell Slade. I started to suspect he'd been taking cocaine in the half-time break.

My half-time had involved enjoying the more acceptable drug, beer, along with an old school friend I'd run into. I'd met Richard, again by chance, at one of Cardiff's Wembley outings (the FA Cup final, I think it was), and I'd never realised he was a Cardiff fan – always nice to meet an unexpected convert. In fairness to him, despite now living in Oxfordshire, he gets to as many games as he can, and I had to sympathise with him after he told me he'd made the trip up to Sunderland last season with his two eldest children, only to witness the humiliating 4-0 defeat. He later recounted this trip to me thus: 'I got the kids up at 4am. They were six and five at the time. I bundled them into the back of the car in their pyjamas with pillows and duvet, drove all the way from Oxfordshire to Sunderland for a lunchtime kick-off in the rain, only to see a 4-0 stuffing, then had to drive them all the way home and try not to get back too late as they had school next day.'

We have a mutual friend, Paul, who lives in Indonesia, and I broke the news to Richard that Paul had got engaged. I joked about how Paul often leaves buying Christmas presents until Christmas Eve, having just returned for the break to his home town of Bridgend. Richard told me he himself did this, one time having to buy all his presents from a petrol station. Definitely something of the Alan Partridge about this, I thought – I've heard people joke about having to do that, but never imagined anyone would have actually done it.

But I digress. Yes, digressions are essential sometimes when the football's not really all that up to it. Disappointing, certainly, but still, I thought Cardiff had reasonable shape with mainstays Whittingham and Gunnarsson putting in good shifts as ever. I heard a song for Whitts as we left the ground to the tune of 'Mrs Robinson', which I'd never heard before. He'd faced criticism at various points over recent seasons, but my view was you couldn't fault his continued committed efforts – he would appear later in the season in a manager's pick of the best starting eleven from the Championship of the last ten years.

So I'd got my football fix, even if it wasn't the greatest game of all time. As we headed for home, Nat let it be known that he'd be back for more – definitely the sign of a true Bluebird in the making if he's willing to go back following a lacklustre display! We arrived back at the Cardiff stadium and I thanked Kevin heartily for letting me travel along with them – although he said it kind of worked out for both of us, my feeling was he'd been by far the kind-hearted one. And in fact, as it turned out, if I'd tried to drive myself, I might never have made it! As I started the engine, it barely got going, and I had to drive home at a snail's pace, some injector fluid clearly needed. Not quite sure why this also made me think of the Cardiff City team? Brrrrmmmm!!

November 29
Watford 0-1 Cardiff: 'You Shall Not Pass!'

'You Shall Not Pass!' Over twenty attempts at goal Watford had, and Cardiff had only a little over twenty per cent possession! No matter – a couple of crunching challenges from Connolly in the first half gave the Watford players a warning, and indeed all Cardiff's backline stayed strong, and henceforth, City's resistance was resilient.

Obviously, it goes without saying that anything the defenders couldn't deal with, once again, our captain proved the saviour, fending off shot after shot. True, many of these were lame, long-range efforts, and Marshall's superpowers were rarely tested to the max. But if Gandalf himself had taken to the pitch, along with staff, his words would not have been needed such was Cardiff's mind-set (though this led to the need to pray that the news of Marshall carrying an injury was either false or exaggerated). The closest Cardiff came to conceding was in fact a 'blue on blue' effort from Turner, but fortunately, his friendly shot fired past the post.

Slade had said a clean sheet was asked for, and that if we were going to win this was all we'd need. He got that spot on, but in the rest of his most recent interview, goals galore he proclaimed he'd accomplished with Orient. Nothing of the sort was on offer here. After the game's solitary goal, which in terms of away goals had been a long time coming, we had no attack to speak of at all. Balls were hoofed forward and possession immediately gifted back to Watford. Forward play was entirely uncoordinated with barely a pass between attackers. At the front, it was more a case of 'We cannot pass!' In the second half, a convincing attack in Watford's half was so rare that it made it difficult to get a photo of City advancing beyond the halfway line.

But City fans sensed that here was a game where the on-pitch performance mattered practically none once the goal was in. The goal itself was a little bizarre. I actually missed it due to texting – totally typical, I know – but having seen the replay, you could see it was almost a parody of a goal. We waited over four hundred minutes for that?!! Le Fondre's tap in from two feet meant it was one of those ones where fans didn't quite know how to celebrate. Look, can you just do it again, the fans seemed to be saying, we didn't do the celebration quite right! Of course, this didn't mean there weren't huge smiles from ear to Cardiff ear.

With every passing moment, the victory line, and Cardiff's first away win of the season – and best of all, in blue – seemed ever closer. It wasn't so much a case of hanging on; not a desperate backline as seen so often under Mackay and Solskjaer, but a newer case of confidence. Despite still looking shabby at times, the team persevered and clung on.

Towards the end, it became ever clearer that a second goal was not really desired – I saw something I don't think I'd ever seen before where a Cardiff corner was taken without a single City player in the Watford penalty box. Even the referee was able to see that we cared not about improving the scoreline, blowing up before a free kick we'd been awarded just outside the box was taken. The joy when that whistle came was written on the face of every fan, to which manager, Slade doffed his cap.

My day had started early. For the first time in my life, I'd boarded a coach to an away match without a ticket, or promise of a ticket, expecting it to be pay on the gate, as apparently it had been for every league game until this one, including Millwalleven. Compadres on the Tony Jeffries coach advised that for some reason tickets would not be on sale for this one, but no problem – St. Vince of Alm was, as ever, to the rescue. By the time I met Vince to pick up the ticket he had for me, after stopping at a pub in Uxbridge for over two hours, I was pretty merry shall we say, and he was probably right in saying they might not have sold me a ticket if they had been on sale.

The merriment on the return journey was pretty much unsurpassed. On the stereo, Queen's 'Don't Stop Me Now' rang out, and we all felt like 'supersonic men' had been made of us. The TIT Travel anthem, 'Sweet Caroline' was broadcast loud and the bus's rendition had to be one of the most euphoric ever. As the bus neared Cardiff, and as Cardiff neared the play-offs, this win was sweet indeed.

December

For some unknown reason, the Bluebirds have never fared particularly well around Christmas time. This season was to be no exception and it turned out to be one of the club's least successful Decembers on record.

I was disappointed not to make the trip to Christina's home town of Bournemouth, though the Bluebirds lost this one as well. From the comfort of bed it sounded like it was a more spirited performance, and must have been exciting with an eventual scoreline of 5-3. Bournemouth, who would go on to win the league, were scoring for fun at this point, and Christina decided to put a lot of small bets on big scorelines, including 20p on 5-3 for a £40 return! The bad news was that there was apparently fighting amongst our own fans over disputes connected to the rebrand.

Things were going so badly for Cardiff, there was even talk now of the possibility of relegation if we continued to play in the same hapless style. To make matters worse still, Vincent Tan delivered a Christmas message warning fans there was nothing they could do to make him change his mind with regard to the rebrand. At this stage, who could have guessed what might be just around the corner?

December 20
Cardiff 2-3 Brentford: Slade Not Christmas No.1

If there was one thing that was guaranteed for this match it was that trade outside the Cardiff City Stadium for blue Santa hats would be brisk. The blue campaign was once again in full effect with some season ticket holders backing a policy of 'No Blue, No Renew'. For non-season ticket holders like myself this season, the club's offer of £10 tickets for this match was a godsend, though it did understandably rile some season ticket holders (is there a shorter expression for this category of fan? Seasoners?), as after all, the reason they hold this type of ticket is to avoid high match-day prices, and this was the second time in twelve matches that this offer had been made. It reflects a lack of numbers when it comes to pay-on-the-day, but sadly, the offer proved to still not be a great incentive with a disappointingly large number of empty seats. The way things had been, some may have felt that even £10 for a miserable afternoon's football was too much – did the club even have to pay people to turn up?!

As it turned out, I enjoyed this one. My own home form had not been that great – after making two of the last three away games, this was the first in three home matches I'd put in an appearance for, so I'd actually looked forward to it.

Christina had bought two red Santa hats, and though I had considered calling a Christmas truce and allowing red objects into the house, I could not be seen at this game with a red hat, so I had to buy a blue one, having given away the one I already had to a friend last Christmas (*'Last Christmas, I gave you my hat…'* Oh dear!). In the stadium there were a variety of blue Santa hats from Christmases of past years – just as with replica shirts, you could try and name the year – ah, the blue Santa hat from the 2004/05 season!

We had yet another problem situation, with the away team, who regularly play in red, having to play in their away strip, in this case yellow, and the west Londoners did not seem overly pleased at watching a team that looked like rivals Watford. You could see that these fans were in party mode, with a string of six red santas in the midst of the away support. Brentford are a team against whom older Bluebirds will recall many a battle when we were struggling in the lower leagues – and they were definitely always one of the stronger teams of third- and fourth-tier football. For some reason, though, it's taken them a long time to win their way into the Championship – if Cardiff found getting promotion to the Premier League problematic, Brentford's efforts to win promotion to this league were in a whole other ball park. No doubt the words Doncaster Rovers have been forcibly removed from the memories of most Bees fans; the mere mention, and they'll be like bees in a hornets' nest, quivering with stress and worry.

For now, clearly these fans were having a ball – newly promoted, and right up there near the top of the table. Respectfully, they sang at us that we should be playing in blue, but it wasn't too long before they instead were jeering that we'd have been better off spending the afternoon Christmas shopping. Within half an hour, the Bluebirds found themselves 3-0 down, and some fans were indeed heading for the exits, even at this early stage in proceedings.

It was a strange half of football in some ways. Brentford were clearly quite a strong side playing with a lot of confidence. And while Cardiff were again struggling to string passes together and looked distinctly amateurish at times, they did actually create a number of chances, and to be quite honest, should have had three goals themselves.

A goal, or clear goalscoring opportunity, was ruled out for no apparent reason – it didn't look to be a foul or an offside; Noone got himself into a good position, but though it was a reasonable effort, for someone who has been considered a possible striker, it perhaps should have been more effective, and then Macheda should have done better with the follow up. Le Fondre had a clear chance, but while he finds scoring from one yard easy, as demonstrated in the Watford game, he seems to struggle with anything beyond two.

The striker position has been problematic for Cardiff City for several seasons. We've been ok at holding teams off, but fulfilling the function of scoring goals – essential to win matches in this sport – and lacking players up front with this ability has let us down. Under Mackay there was Miller, often a lone striker, who once went, I believe, over ten games without scoring. Next there was Campbell who, although supposed to score 'go-o-o-o-oals', did not really fulfil potential, and let's not even talk about performances under Solskjaer's reign. Finally, now there was the Le Fondre/Macheda partnership, which really was not working, with just two goals each in the previous ten games.

At half-time, most talk was about damage limitation – preventing a further flood of Brentford goals. Surely only a Christmas miracle could assist this lacklustre Cardiff side in turning round a 3-0 deficit? One thing was for sure – changes were needed.

City began the second half brighter, and they were quickly rewarded with a goal from Craig Noone. In fairness, this was one of Noone's best displays – he did not stop running and looking to be part of things for the whole game. Home fans, sensing possibilities, perked up. Brentford were quieter this half – the team hardly needed to be all guns blazing after all, only needing to contain us if they were content with their own goal tally.

Cardiff's outlook seemed to have changed, but real change in the form of different personnel was clearly also called for, and it was not long before Jones was on for Macheda. Jones offered a different style, a little bit more aggressive, but was not necessarily a better prospect when goals were needed. Nonetheless, fortunately, a further goal did come from his boot on seventy-five minutes, and with the scoreline at 3-2, it seemed just possible that City could just get something from this.

Brentford remained quiet – barely a shot in the first half – and clearly containing, which was surprising. But despite our 2 goals, we didn't really make this job too difficult for the away team. Far, far too often, like a lazy, lower-league team, Cardiff players launched the ball forward hopefully, and every single time, Brentford defenders simply picked the ball up, and took it back to us. Did this team, which still had a few players from last year's Premier League outfit, really not have the ability to pass it around on the turf? The answer, many times in this game, was no – far too many relatively short and easy passes were not being completed, making it easy for the opposing side. Basics, lads, basics!

Despite getting two back, frustration from home fans was telling. Once again, the situation was not helped by fans not getting properly behind the team. It's all very well moaning about the team's performance, or moaning at the manager, but what happened to the twelfth man in terms of vocal support? Of course things weren't great, but come on, give the team a break!

It amazed me that Slade had managed four home wins from four, and had now just lost the first in six, and people were calling for him to be gone. The football hadn't been wonderful, and the away form was pretty poor, but couldn't fans give him a chance? After all, this was a team that Slade himself had had very little part in putting together – give him the chance to get his own players in over Christmas was my thinking. There were some fans still ruing the missed chance of installing Pulis as manager. We had to forget Pulis! Honestly, if Cardiff went back to blue, there would be some fans saying it was the wrong shade of blue!

I wondered about Slade's message that he was going to get the team fit. In this match the players did not stop running until the end. Even in stoppage time they still kept going. Kadeem Harris, who looked a tiny bit out of his depth, still had the energy to put in a good striking effort with minutes to go, and Whitts also had a go in the dying moments. However, although all the players looked capable of running until the end, the general tempo throughout the match was a little slow. There were players like Brayford and Noone who could practically run a marathon at a sprint, but the rest seemed content to go through the match at middle-distance rate, which was something that looked like it needed working on.

Possibly the most worrying thing about this match was a possible slip in form from Marshall. He had after all now let in eight goals in two games. Not sure if he was at fault for too many of the goals against Bournemouth but in this game I did think he might have done better for Brentford's first, and on better form, could even have got a hand to the third. We all know that Marshall was one of the main reasons we got promotion and often carried the side. We've played poorly many times, but just clung on to a 1-0 win many a time due to Marshall, without whom many of those games we'd be losing 3-1. If Marshall started making mistakes and conceding, Cardiff really could be in trouble – and there was still the question of whether he had a slight injury.

So the Christmas miracle did not happen – and all we got was to see a slightly less punishing scoreline. If Christmas is a good time for reflection, at approximately the halfway stage in the season, Cardiff could reflect that improvement was still needed in many areas. We knew we were not the best team in the league so we could expect a few defeats against the teams at the top, but on the other hand, if we were going to still fight for a play-off spot we definitely needed to improve performances against teams below us. Faith in Slade had to be maintained for the time being at least was my thinking, even if, on this occasion, he did not give everyone a Merry Xmas.

December 28
Cardiff 2-4 Watford: The Nightmare After Christmas

Total nightmare: could there be a better phrase to sum up this performance? Utter shite maybe? Had Cardiff ever in their history produced a worse set of results around Christmas time than this? I seriously doubt it. Three defeats and one draw in four games, with thirteen goals conceded – that does not look good on paper, and looked even worse on the pitch. Even the drawn game was against ten men for over half of the match. Two points from fifteen in December was pretty woeful.

This was now a Cardiff side that was playing without skill, without ambition, without pace and, most of the time, without the ball, because when they had it, they appeared as eager as possible to get rid of it, and when they didn't have it, they showed reluctance to try and retrieve it.

As fans were stepping up plans to protest I was starting to wonder if the Cardiff players had launched their own campaign and that playing shit was their method of approach. But was it a campaign against Tan or against us, the fans? Maybe they'd grown tired of the silence that greeted them at home games – perhaps they thought that with fans so focussed on other matters, we didn't care about the quality of the football on show?

What players were perhaps not aware of, however, is that once inside the soul-sapping stadium, with not much going on in the crowd, there is little to do but focus on the football. If anything, the game is now over-scrutinised, with every fan now willing to impart their critique of the performance, every kick or tackle is cross-examined. The crowd is more transfixed on watching the game than ever before, so when they're served up garbage of this sort, it really is no wonder that the reaction is not positive. These are fans who have endured shocking performances in the Premier leading to relegation in one season, and were now witnessing equally dire football in the Championship, which somehow had allowed us to just about stay in the top half of the table, while the home team was playing in the wrong coloured kit, and we were expected to pay a walk-up price of £30 for the privilege of watching. Understandably disgruntled?

It wasn't fun being in the stands, put it that way. The morgue-like atmosphere continued, with fans seemingly almost fearful to open their mouths before the designated time of 19:27. Enduring twenty minutes of silence up until this time was a painful experience. Just before the 19 minute mark in this game Cardiff were awarded a free kick and scored just as Cardiff fans were lifting their blue scarves by way of protestation, and so suddenly the gesture became one of celebration, but it was still a little confusing. Fans really did not seem overwhelmingly optimistic that this early lead would aid the team in winning the match, so proved to be the case, and we were 2-1 down at the break.

During the half-time interval, in the foyer, some people tried to get a couple of chants going, as if they felt that if it wasn't going to happen above them in the stands, they were going to have to try it downstairs in the interval. I think just two songs were achieved, which were admittedly quite loud, but still even this effort was a little forced and lacking in gusto.

When Watford banged in their third goal I almost thought about applauding. Very rarely will I actually applaud an away team's goal, sometimes I might do it ironically, and just occasionally, for genuine reasons. This one was one of the best goals I'd ever seen in a live game: a shot delivered like a lightning bolt, thumped into the back of the net, as if punishing Cardiff. That was the second time in two games the opposing side had scored a wonder goal against us – Charlton's equaliser at The Valley being as impressive – and there was almost a case to go and watch Cardiff at the time, not to follow our own exploits, but to marvel at the opposition.

City had already made two not particularly inspiring substitutions, and not long after Watford's third goal, a third change in personnel was effected, with Macheda coming on for Le Fondre. Personally, I didn't know whether to laugh or cry; the switch was met by extremely muted applause, and I honestly can't believe that those who were clapping were doing so in praise of either the merits of the player leaving the pitch, or for his replacement.

Slade was once again coming in for some stick, but I didn't

think he could be criticised too much for his choice of substitutes: who else did he have on offer? Could anyone honestly say that there was one Cardiff player who had been sidelined for any length of time who, if brought into the side, could seriously improve things? It was hardly the case that the starting 11 was so impeccable that it shouldn't be meddled with, but until Slade was given the chance to buy his own players, his choice of team could not be questioned too much. With over ten games under his belt it might finally have been permissible to query his tactics and to question just what kind of lacklustre training regime was allowing performances of this standard to keep occurring.

There was not one player in this game who stood out as someone who really showed any inspiration; even Craig Noone was kept quiet. Le Fondre for once was running around a bit, but still showed little in front of goal, making a mess of one opportunity he had early on to put City two goals up. He may be down as scorer of the first, but his contribution was pretty meagre, the ball glancing off his head goalwards.

There was barely a player who played with any flair. We desperately needed a form striker to regularly start knocking in goals. We needed players behind him to be playing with confidence and conviction. Along with much better individual displays, we needed a team that could play comfortably together. We needed more entertainment – and only then might the crowd be lifted.

What made things worse was that this Watford side did not look particularly like any great shakes: there was not the class of the Brentford team that put 3 past us in the first half eight days before. Prior to the start of this game, a friend had been hopeful we would achieve our first double of the season after we'd somehow, against the odds, beaten Watford in our first away win of the season at the end of November. In that game Watford had enjoyed all the possession as they inflicted a tirade of attacks on the Cardiff defence. At least then Cardiff had shown a resilient spirit. This time Watford were far more keen to make amends than allow Cardiff the chance of a double.

When Watford scored their fourth, this understandably led to a mass walkout of the home crowd. I'm not someone who will very often leave early, but on this occasion, I really did not feel like sticking around, and was not too disappointed to have missed Kenwyne Jones' late consolation.

With Cardiff nine points from the play-off places, and eleven points above the relegation zone, it was looking likely that if we weren't playing in the Championship in the following season, the prospect of League 1 football was looking far more likely than promotion.

Tan's Christmas Statement

Like the Queen addressing the nation, on Christmas Day Vincent Tan felt the need to address Cardiff City fans. The main reason for this was to respond to the announcement from Cardiff supporters groups that fans would be staging two fresh protests in the New Year against Tan's ill-fated rebrand.

His main argument was that he had agreed to invest in the club on the condition that the colour of the strip and the club badge was changed, therefore fans were not honouring the other side of the bargain by demanding that the change be reversed. There were two main faults with this argument as I saw it. The first was that the rebrand was made without the full support of all fans – the club's board may have agreed, but a good number of fans did not.

The second point, and for me the most crucial point, was that it had become quite apparent that the rebrand had not been a success, so why keep to it, regardless of the money invested? From a commercial point of view, and for Tan to actually improve on his investment, it surely made sense to return to blue? The club could not have been doing much trade in red shirts as nobody wanted to wear them. A return to blue would no doubt mean they would do a roaring trade. Traders outside of the stadium selling blue hats and scarves were surely faring better.

But even more significantly Tan surely had to see that he had caused a great deal of hurt and discomfort for fans, and how ridiculous it had become that the team was playing in one colour, while the fans were wearing another.

In interviews Tan seemed to want to try and sideline the issue and concentrate on other matters. But for fans it was *the* main issue. Two seasons ago, due to the fact that Cardiff fans, having strived for so long, were desperate for promotion to the Premier League, the desire for success was more of a focus. However, even then, large numbers of fans were still campaigning throughout the season for the rebrand to be reversed.

This season, promotion was definitely a secondary concern. Performances by the team indicated that promotion was a long shot at best, but even in spite of this, this season, if it came down to it, I think fans would actually have taken a reversal of the rebrand over promotion.

Tan himself might have realised that promotion was becoming less likely. Prior to the start of the season he did state that if we won promotion he could then consider a compromise. This angered fans at the time as it was hoped that as we'd been relegated, the one thing that the club could do for the 2014/15 season would be to go back to blue. It seemed the sensible thing to do but the opportunity was missed and we had to endure the prospect of yet another season in the wrong colour.

I think there was one point that stuck out for me which made the whole issue the more absurd, and that was the club's nickname. Leave aside history and tradition and whether Tan may have forsaken these. There have been countless examples of businesses trying to modernise and attempting a rebranding process. Perhaps part of the problem was that this particular rebrand was not about modernising but a change of image, introducing the dragon emblem to reinforce the Welsh aspect of the club, etc. But the nickname of the club, the Bluebirds was never changed.

Of course, for fans to agree to that would have taken a gargantuan effort. But what was always said at the time the idea of the rebrand was being introduced was that Cardiff City would be given a new strip and that it would still be Cardiff City playing on the pitch. The nickname used by fans, the media, by everyone when referring to Cardiff City was not considered. It may have been suggested that the nickname could be changed, perhaps to the Cardiff Dragons, or something like that, but it was never done. For the first few weeks of Cardiff's first season in red nobody was really sure how Cardiff should be referred to. But it was quite quickly realised that we were still the Bluebirds. It sounded distinctly odd for a while, but it was now very much established. We were the Bluebirds but we play in red. This for me was the crucial problem, and was one of the main reasons why the rebrand failed and needed to be reversed.

So now Tan was saying that he was going to ignore the proposed protests and it would not make him change his mind. In response, fans said that the protests would still go ahead. It appeared now to be a large number of people against one man, his stubbornness and his pride. For many, like myself, at the time, I think if Tan could have just agreed to go back to blue, we would have been happy for him to continue as the owner of the club. But as Tan now appeared to be completely digging his heels in, and ignoring what everyone was saying, my thoughts at this point were that he would have to go.

He had become more distant, he had completely alienated fans, many of whom were now disillusioned with the club. He had created a very unpleasant situation and he was not willing to do the one thing that could change this. Despite his generosity when it came to money he was like Scrooge in many ways, not willing to change his ways – if he had just had a Scrooge-like revelation – perhaps if he was shown the ghosts of Cardiff City Past, Present and Future – perhaps he might come to his senses and help out Cardiff fans, instead of continuing his campaign against us. He was distant in the literal sense; no longer actually attending matches. Was he actually fearful to attend the stadium which he had put all this money into? How sad a situation was that?

There was speculation of a consortium that had plans to buy Tan out, and this consortium would of course return Cardiff to blue. If there were people who had the money to do this it did seem that this was the only way the situation could be resolved. I felt some regret that this now seemed the only viable option. Tan came to the club, he gave us a helping hand and we reached the Premier. He had a vision to change things. But when this vision palpably had been shown to be unpopular it seemed desperately sad that one man's pride and reluctance to back down and change his mind should be the one thing that should prevent him from continuing. The change hinged on the investment of £100 million and now it seemed that it would take a pay-out of £100 million for things to change back. There had been talk all the way through of the soul of Cardiff City having been sold. It seemed now that that there was only one option left, and that was, to buy it back.

Section 2:

The Battle For Blue: Looking Back on Two and a Half Years of Protest

'Blue is the male principle, stern and spiritual. Yellow the female principle, gentle, cheerful and sensual. Red is matter, brutal and heavy and always the colour which must be fought and vanquished by the other two.'

FRANZ MARC

The manner in which the rebrand of Cardiff City came about can be compared to the outbreak of World War II in some respects. When Vincent Tan first made the suggestion that he would like to change the colour of the club's home kit and its badge, this caused a bit of a furore, particularly amongst fans, but after consultation, like Chamberlain returning with his letter of appeasement, it was announced that the rebrand would not after all be going ahead. There followed a period of backtracking, rapid withdrawal of racist remarks that had been made, and sucking up to Tan due to the fact that after all, everyone still welcomed his proposed investment of £100 million. Tan then decided that in spite of initially holding off, sensing that he now had the backing of fans, like Hitler going into Poland, he would after all go ahead with the rebrand, effectively declaring war on Cardiff City fans.

Or so it was thought. I think a good number of Cardiff fans just assumed that all fans would be against Tan's plan. I think most fans assumed that, immediately after it was first announced that the rebrand would be going ahead, which was a month or so prior to the start of the 2012/2013 season, there would still be time for Tan to change his mind back again. But in fact, Tan had sufficient backing from a select group of fans which in the event proved crucial.

On July 24, 2012, a meeting of fans was called at The Municipal Club on City Road, Cardiff. This meeting was chaired by a campaign group calling itself Keep Cardiff Blue. It was all very honourable, except nobody exactly knew who this group was, and then at the meeting itself, it turned out the group was headed by Scott Thomas of the London-based supporters group, the 1927 Club. This club had always been respected by Cardiff fans (though it has since been disbanded), but people had become so used to regular supporters group representatives that seeing this hitherto unknown fan attempting to announce himself as representing fans might have surprised some.

I attended this meeting and I thought he spoke well, and with passion. There were probably around 80-100 fans in attendance, including some quite well-known fans. Various people were given a chance to speak. I chipped in with quite a heartfelt argument on why I was totally against the change. Part of my little speech was quoted in the *Echo*'s report on the meeting: 'What this meeting demonstrates is both sides of Cardiff City. We have always had a lot of fighting spirit. We should have been protesting all throughout the summer and should have had a permanent protest outside the ground. I don't think this is one of the worst things to happen to Cardiff City, I think it is one of the worst things to ever happen in football.'

Sadly, this meeting lacked proper cohesion, and had no solid intentions as to how to progress. The meeting became further unhinged by the presence of one particular prominent

Cardiff fan, Gwyn Davies, formerly of the much respected Valley Rams, accompanied by two of his cronies. Gwyn cuts quite a formidable figure in terms of body stature alone, and his friends equally do not look like people to mess with. Gwyn threw in a totally unexpected curveball, in a meeting which was expected to be all about opposing the rebrand, by announcing that he essentially was backing Tan's proposals. Gwyn's argument was that we should back Tan because of the promised investment. He wanted to see Cardiff City promoted and that it would still be Cardiff City playing regardless of the colour of the kit. He suggested opposing the rebrand would disrupt Cardiff's push for promotion and he was not about to allow that to happen. He continued in a disruptive manner, forcing the meeting to eventually wind up without any proper conclusions having been made.

Fans on the opposite side of the room to Gwyn, which included myself, frequent drinking buddy Carl and a couple of his friends who were vehemently against the rebrand and were discussing action to take to oppose it, were appalled at all of this. As far as we saw it, the history of the club was being disrespected and disregarded. We were very much in the anti-red camp from the offset, the irony being that we might have been considered on the left side in terms of our politics and our anti-authoritarian attitude.

In the middle of the room stood Annis Abraham, who I believe had not long returned from a summer holiday. Say what you like about him, and many people have said many things, in my mind, Annis is one of the truest Cardiff City fans of all. Yes, he has been involved in trouble in the past, but so too were a great number of Cardiff fans – that's how things used to be. In more recent years Annis has been at the forefront of all kinds of campaigns which look out for fans.

Annis always has Cardiff City at the forefront of his mind, and what is best for its supporters.

So Annis was always there, and this was a campaign which he clearly had a lot of interest in. But at this meeting, Annis himself stayed unusually quiet. I think he sensed that this was perhaps one of the biggest issues that the club had ever been faced with. I think he felt that he did not want to immediately respond. He had for so long always been at the forefront – all the responsibility had been placed on his shoulders. He had listened to both sides of the argument, and I think he thought, you know what, just for once, let's see how this one pans out. Let's see if these other fans can for once settle it themselves. Intentionally or not, at the meeting, Annis was wearing purple. Since the meeting Annis has been firmly in the blue camp, wearing blue to every Cardiff match. If he had just spoken out at that meeting, things may have gone differently, but perhaps he felt, why should it always need me to settle things?

And so the meeting was disbanded. If anything, the meeting had probably come too late anyway. The time for proper protest might have been in the couple of weeks leading up to the meeting – as I'd said, we should have already staged a protest at the ground. I had thought of doing this, along with many other things, but perhaps like Annis, in a way, I'd thought, why me? Why should it be me doing this, pulling some kind of stunt? Did I want to be known as the stunt man? Are there not other fans to take up the mantle, I thought, or better still, shouldn't we all protest as one, rather than individual fans doing their own thing individually? There were online campaigns, and a lot of words spoken online, but these never seem to have the same impact as a more traditional form of protest.

There was talk of protests and campaigns of action. There was further outcry right up until the start of the season, but in that month leading up to the first game, things actually quietened down, and in fact, there was not even a proper formal protest at the first game. It was a bizarre opening game, one which Cardiff were very lucky to come away from with a 1-0 win, but far more bizarre for most fans was watching our club, who we had always watched in blue, now playing in red. I think it stunned people into silence. People did not know what to sing, many of the familiar songs centring on our being blue, now seemingly inappropriate.

On the pitch, Cardiff under Malky Mackay had a good season, without ever playing spectacular football. David Marshall was instrumental in ensuring that we won many games where the opposing side could have scored to level things or go in front. Ironically, at away games, where we played in our new blue away strip, we seemed to leak goals badly, leading some to even start speculating that Tan's claim that red was lucky could be true. I went to Bristol City away, which was a virtual sell-out, but I turned up at the stadium first thing in the morning before the Supporters coaches left, and good old Vince Alm, chairman of the Supporters Club, so often a saviour in these situations, was on hand to let me have a ticket. I didn't want to miss this one as it would be our first away game in our new reserve strip of blue, due to the fact that, obviously, Bristol play in red. I couldn't believe there were still one or two people who were going to this match in the new red kit. That game was disappointing for me. Now, even our away support was not as passionate as it once was, and Bristol I felt, with their old-fashioned ground, and old-fashioned fans, completely outsung us. I can't quite remember what happened on the pitch – I think we were well beaten.

But our seemingly lacklustre support was by far the more worrying thing for me – things had been like this for a while, long before the rebrand.

But the whole thing with the rebrand was truly preposterous. For me, one of the most frustrating factors was that Tan had never expressly said exactly why he wanted Cardiff to change to red. Sam Hammam had wanted to change the colour of the strip, possibly to red, white, and green, like the Welsh flag (he more sensibly backed down at the request of fans), and Tan has also said that to enhance Cardiff's status as a global team, one that is recognised for being Welsh, a change to red would be better. But while everybody knows that the Welsh national side plays in red, surely Cardiff as a club team should protect its own individual identity? The most prominent English sides do not play in white, after all. The idea of Arsenal, Chelsea, Liverpool or Man Utd changing to white because they're English would be viewed as absurd. People speculated that Tan wanted Cardiff to look more like Man Utd but we didn't want that. Perhaps it was to do with a new sponsor? No proper reason has ever been given, and it increasingly came to be seen as having been done at the whim of a rich owner.

Throughout the season, people continued to argue that it was still Cardiff City. The argument that they would still watch Cardiff City play in pink polka dots if it meant promotion was often spoken of. But there was something else people were missing. And that was, if it is still Cardiff City, are we also still the Bluebirds? While the kit had been changed, and it may have been suggested we could be dubbed the Dragons or something similar, officially, the club nickname was never changed. The media, who often prefer to use club nicknames, did not know what to do. Fans didn't know what to do. The bluebird, though now much smaller, and beneath the dragon on the new, very much disliked, club crest, was still there. So people continued to call Cardiff the Bluebirds, despite the fact that at home, we wore red. This made things truly ridiculous.

For a lot of fans there was pride at stake. There was a danger that Cardiff could be considered a laughing stock for having 'sold out'. Premier League Swansea were having a whale of a time, joking on message boards that we were Tan's ladyboys, and just what were we now, the red Malaysian Cardiff City Dragonbirds? We had no clear identity. We feared that every visiting club's fans would have a joke at our expense, and we did not have a good way of defending ourselves. The truth was that opposing fans perhaps did not mock us as much as we might have expected, but it still seemed a little shameful.

In an attempt to appease fans, large boards were placed around the foyers and bars in the Ninian Stand, the Canton Stand and the Grandstand showing photos of City's most significant historic wins and players. But the ridiculous thing, of course, was that all of these showed Cardiff players in blue, and yet we were now in red. Step into the Family Stand, and here the real horror of the situation was laid bare for all to see. Red everywhere here, with large cuddly cartoon players in red, as if this was training for the next generation to accept red as the future.

But as long as we were still doing well in the league, people were still not kicking up too much of a fuss. Early in 2013, Tan announced that the club would be dishing out free red scarves to everyone who attended the Brighton game in February. I'd had a couple of pints prior, not looking forward to this game one bit, and as a result only got to the ground just as the match was getting underway, and by this time, all the free scarves had gone. Not that I wanted one – I'm not sure what I'd have done with it if I had been given it, but one thing was for sure, I certainly had no plans to wear one. Unlike the vast majority of the crowd who put the scarf on seemingly without a second thought. This was not at all what people on the message boards, for example, had hoped for. There had been the hope that this night might turn into more of a protest, but no, acceptance was the guiding principle. I saw just one or two scarves that had been thrown onto the pitch, when it had been expected that far more would be discarded in protest.

Throughout all of this, my position was one of continued resistance. I felt desperately sad about the whole thing. Once it was pretty much apparent that the rebrand was going ahead, it was constantly on my mind that this was wrong, potentially damaging to the club, whether or not we had the extra money, and I was forever thinking of ways to demonstrate my intolerance to the situation. One of the first things I did before the start of the first season in red was to walk from my home in Roath to Cardiff's stadium in Canton carrying a mug I'd bought some years before with the words 'I heart (love) Cardiff City' on it. Not exactly a long walk, but still, kind of symbolic. Once I got to the stadium, I walked into the reception and spoke to the receptionist. I spoke to her about how the writing of the words were in blue, and for a reason. That the heart was red, for a reason. I told her that if Cardiff changed to red, I could no longer love the club, and I then left the mug with her, and walked out. A pretty silly thing to do, especially as it was my favourite mug – a very nice shape to drink out of – but I suppose it was just one very small sacrifice on my behalf. The significance for me on a personal basis was that this was the first symbolic act in my continued resistance to the rebrand.

I had had a season ticket the season before, but for the first season in red, I did not renew. Part of the reason I'd had a season ticket in the 2011/12 season was that we had re-signed Robert Earnshaw, one of my favourite players, but for some unknown reason, he was hardly ever picked, and what with the rebrand, I really did not feel like getting a season ticket for the 2012/13 season. By Christmas time, with results going very well, with Cardiff top of the table and looking like a very good bet for promotion, I did then buy a half-season ticket, expecting I would need one of these to be entitled to get a season ticket for our first season in the Premier, although as it turned out, I didn't then renew after all, as I felt the price for Premier League tickets was just too high.

In the 2012/13 season, I quite often went to a small bar in Canton before the match – the Potters Bar it was known as then – which had become quite popular with a lot of fans. Carl's friends who'd been at the meeting before the start of the season were often there. They along with many others were also continuing with their plan of sustained resistance. They had made blue stickers with the words 'Keep Cardiff Blue' on them, and let me have a few to distribute myself. I put them around a few places, and then went back to them to try and get more, but as they never had many on them I got my own made, even copying the design more or less exactly.

I put these around all kinds of places. I decided that every time I went past the Cardiff City shop in town, where, of course, most of the merchandise was now red, I would place one outside the front of the shop. Of course, whenever I went back there, it would have been taken down, but then, I'd just put up another. Even if it only stayed up for an hour or two, or until the shop closed, if any passers-by saw it even just for a moment, I'd be happy that this may have had a small influence when it came to their decision as to whether or not to buy red merchandise.

As for the red scarf, I did half wish I had one, if only for the purposes of using it in a form of protest. I wanted to burn one, that's what I really wanted to do. I ended up actually buying one from Carl (who'd somehow acquired three of them) for the price of a drink, I think it was. But I never quite carried through with what I'd intended. One time, late at night, I did drive to the stadium with the scarf, with the intention of setting it alight, perhaps next to the old Ninian Park gates, outside the stadium. I suppose I would have filmed myself doing it. But somehow I couldn't bring myself to do it. Again, I suppose the thought process was – why should it be me doing this? Maybe if I'd had an accomplice there with me, it may have been different, but for whatever reason, I didn't go through with it.

I think there were many people who felt like doing similar things, but you never really got to hear of it, as people were no doubt reluctant to discuss such things in public on the message boards, the best source of information on all things Cardiff City for most people. I know for a fact that, despite the 'Night of the Red Scarf', there were still many people against it. In some ways, at this stage, the protest was going a bit more underground – the actual group, Keep Cardiff Blue, which never really had proper support in the first place, was now not very popular. But it was a bit like the People's Front of Judea fighting the Judea People's Front. We were mostly against the rebrand, but as we were not united against it as such, there was a bit of in-fighting.

Certainly however, as Cardiff's push for promotion was staying very much intact, there could be no denying that this became much more of a focus for a while. But that is not to say that people were still not against the rebrand, and there was still a dislike of Tan for having been the instigator. Even at the very last home match, when we had gained promotion to the Premier, the prize for which we'd strived for so long, when Tan took to the pitch, there were people shouting abuse at him. I suppose the thinking was, we've reached the Premier League after all this time, and now when we get there, we won't even be playing in blue! It did seem pretty absurd.

Throughout all this time, there were those that had just accepted the rebrand, they bought the red merchandise, in the same way that they bought the new strip every season. You can't really fault this type of fan too much – it was still Cardiff City, as many people kept reiterating. And yet, there were many who did not see it as Cardiff City. There were some who did the exact opposite, by returning season tickets, and staying away from the ground. It was so far removed from their notion of what the football club was that they could no longer support it. There were people then at both extremes.

Going into our Premier League year, it was clear that there would still be no let-up in the campaign to return to blue. The two main message boards were not rebranded, and remained blue. Everyone on the message boards who had the word blue in their username – Annis for example, is Forever Blue – kept their usernames. The resistance was ongoing despite the success of the club in terms of gaining promotion. The message boards were the main places for online campaigns – one user, known as Barry Chuckles, organised a petition, which I believe had quite a large number of signatures.

It always seemed that for every action the club took to

reinforce the rebrand, there would be fans to counteract it. Every time something was done at the stadium – the new badge put up, for example, or red fittings installed – fans would be up in arms. There was talk of the seats being changed from blue to red, and this really would have been the pits for many fans, although at the same time, of course, people did see that as long as we played at home in red with a blue stadium, it was always going to look pretty odd. At the start of the 2014/15 season, when a new stand was installed, these seats were red, but luckily, the club saw sense to never change the colour of the seats in the rest of the stadium.

When the 2013/14 season started, and fans were having to face the prospect of playing in the Premier for the first time – but, as many saw it, in the wrong colour – one group got some money together to pay for a billboard right near to the stadium, with the words 'Bluebirds Unite: History, Identity, Pride'. I have to say, I saw this as an excellent effort on their part. It was perfectly positioned so that Cardiff City officials could see it, and it was really one in the eye to Tan and the Cardiff board of directors, giving a clear message that even in this Premier League year, we as fans were not going to just accept things.

It became clear quite early on that this was not going to be a successful foray into the Premier League. There were some high points to begin with, such as beating Man City, but by Christmas time, our manager, Malky Mackay, was out, and his replacement, Solskjaer, did not look like he was going to turn things around. In spite of what's emerged more recently, the sacking of Malky Mackay was not popular amongst fans, despite the fact that the football had not been the best. It gave people another excuse to have a go at Tan. In fact, just about anything that went wrong at the club was blamed on Tan, when a lot of the time, it was just fans taking out their frustration with regard to the rebrand. Tan became almost like a comedy villain. He had wanted Cardiff City to become well known, but if anything, this was now being achieved for the wrong reasons.

The protests were being stepped up, and a couple of formal protests were arranged. The biggest of these involved thousands of Cardiff fans marching to the ground, in blue, by way of demonstration. Annis was at the forefront of this, and again, you couldn't fault his commitment. We made a lot of noise – much more than we were making at that time inside the ground – but it did seem almost as if it was falling on deaf ears. But there were thousands of people there – I was amongst them – and it really felt like at last it was making sense; that at last the fans were coming together in unity. Tan had referred to those against the rebrand as being in a very small minority, but we were showing now that, in fact, the opposite was true – that those against the rebrand were in a clear majority.

A car approached the ground during this protest with a number plating seeming to indicate that it might be Tan himself. One fan approached the car and I think looked into it. People turned around but he then shouted out that it wasn't Tan in the car. I later saw footage of the car driving right up to the entrance and Tan getting out and going into the building. If the fan who'd looked in had indeed seen Tan and let people know, the car might have been mobbed. Tan needed to tread carefully. I think what Tan never quite realised was just how much a football club can mean to people; it's almost as if it gets into your soul, and the identity is very important. Tan was potentially making a large number of people really quite miserable – many times, I honestly felt as if I had a kind of sickness.

Still, no announcement was forthcoming that the rebrand would be reversed and fans' frustration was ongoing. It now became very much the trend to wear blue at matches, and people wearing red were becoming scarce. Merchandise stalls inside the ground selling only red merchandise were starting to look laughable – no-one was buying it! It started to become clear that even from a commercial point of view, the rebrand had been ineffective. The atmosphere inside the ground was still not good, but one thing that fans did begin to do was hold up blue scarves at a designated point in the match, that being on 19 minutes, 27 seconds, 1927 after all being the number that connects all Cardiff City fans. Personally, I've never been keen on these kind of staged events at football matches – I'd prefer fans to be singing throughout spontaneously – but if Tan took notice, I suppose it might help.

Once it was clear that we were heading for relegation, I suppose a lot of fans thought that now finally Tan might see sense and return us to blue. We were having to drop back to the Championship after just one season in the top flight, Swansea were staying up, enjoying their time there, the least Tan could do, you might think, would be to make the change?

Instead, he maintained his stance. He made quite a ridiculous statement saying that if we returned to the Premier then he might look at what he could do in terms of a possible compromise. This was madness. He was basically saying that we would have to endure yet another season in red, and that even at the end of the season, unless we were going back to the Premier League we would still stay in red. It made no sense, and only served to incense fans still further.

My own resistance continued with a vengeance. I announced on Annis' message board that I would be banning the colour red from my house. I was tending to favour this message board over the older fans' message board as to me it was more football-based, whereas the other one, while funnier, has a lot of non-football related posts and in-jokes (the official Cardiff City message board on the official site never really took off – indeed, I don't even know if it's still running).

I suppose my plan to have a non-red flat was a bit of a joke in a sense, but it was something I could do to show that I, along with many other fans, would be continuing with the campaign. I did have one party where I got drunk and threw quite a lot of stuff out, but I must admit, there were certain things, like a red blanket, that I then recovered from outside the house once sober. It kind of fizzled out in a way, although I always said that in the spring I would continue banishing more things if necessary.

One time, I was in the Andrew Buchan bar on Albany Road. Here they serve one of the best pints in Cardiff, Rhymney Export, at a very good price. There was a fair bit of Cardiff City memorabilia around the place. At the start of the 2013/14 season, they started selling a Premier Ale, which I think was just their regular bitter rebranded. It had the cringeworthy new Cardiff badge on, so of course, I avoided this – I'm not sure if John the owner actually realised that this would prove unpopular. On one wall there was a stag's head with a red scarf on one antler and a blue scarf on the other. One time, after a few pints, as I was leaving the bar, I grabbed the red scarf and threw it onto the fireplace below. One of the staff grabbed it quickly so that it didn't burn just as I made my exit. I was sure I'd be banned for this, but fortunately, I don't think word ever got back to the owner, who had a reputation for banning people even for very minor things.

When the NATO summit came to town in September 2014, with a large fence erected around the periphery of the castle (I did wonder why a castle with walls several metres wide needed extra protection), I planned to spray paint 'Keep Cardiff Blue' on the fence. This was another of my schemes that I was a bit wary of doing, but in the end, I did manage to spray paint it on a wall near to the fence, despite a large police presence. By the morning it was pretty much gone, although the words 'iff Blue' could still just be seen for a short time.

In November, I decided that what I could do to finally get the scarf burned was make a guy for bonfire night, wrap him in the scarf and burn the guy. My girlfriend, Christina, even suggested that we make it a Vincent Tan guy, and put his face on it. I was a bit unsure – was this going too far? – but she spent a fair bit of time making the guy, and it was quite impressive in the end. We took it out onto the streets to parade it, asking for a penny for the guy in the traditional manner. We didn't raise much cash – some people literally giving just a penny! – but I suppose that wasn't the intention. Someone else happened to have an art display on Queen Street that day, featuring, incredibly enough, a red carpet and some red curtains, so we took some photos of our Tan Guy next to this. A few other people also took photos, and it generally went down quite well.

I had thought of then burning it in the back garden, but it was a slightly damp bonfire night, and in the end, we took it to the firework display in Rhiwbina where one of the firefighters then unceremoniously threw it onto their large bonfire. Within seconds, the guy which Christina had spent quite some time making was up in flames, but I suppose that's what we'd wanted. The scarf was finally burned!

At games, people continued to wear blue, and the 19:27 protest was now a regular part of every game, with fans all around the ground raising their blue and white scarves, and singing 'We'll always be blue'. Even away fans often chanted their support of the blue campaign (although there was also still some hostility). There were now hardly any people wearing red, and there surely could not have been many people buying the red merchandise. Everyone said that if the club went back to blue now, shirts would probably fly out.

The season didn't start well on the pitch, Solskjaer was sacked, and Slade brought in, after a short-term interim management team of Scott Young and Danny Gabbidon. Slade got a few results to begin with, but then we had a disastrous December, and promotion now was looking like a pipedream. If Tan was not going to return to blue unless we made the Premier League, it didn't look like that was going to happen, so it was felt that efforts to persuade him to return to blue regardless would have to be stepped up.

A lot of people were saying that they would not renew their season tickets unless we went back to blue. The case for maintaining red seemed increasingly implausible from a commercial point of view, aside from anything else. Surely, fans felt, Tan must see sense and do the decent thing? It did seem as if it was only his pride or stubbornness that prevented him from backtracking on his ill-fated decision. He made an announcement on Christmas Day that he was not for turning, and this led to fans arranging protests for the New Year.

I had proposed a Christmas Day truce, and suggested, half in jest, that fans should permit themselves to allow red into their homes for one day only as, after all, although many fans have blue Santa hats, it's pretty difficult to escape red at Christmas. After Tan's statement, I once again felt more serious about the blue campaign. It did seem now that the only way we were going to go back to blue was if Tan left (which had been the calling of other fans for some time), was bought out or forced out. There was talk of a consortium to buy him out, but this seemed unlikely. The protests were going to have to go ahead.

But then, unexpectedly, the club called a meeting to allow fans to have their say, which came a little out of the blue. There was not an official boycott, but many stayed away from the FA Cup game against Colchester (I couldn't make it as I had a friend's engagement party to go to), and maybe the low attendance finally forced their hand, the very last straw in terms of the club coming to a realisation that things could not go on as they were.

Tan, who had not come to watch a match all season, was not present at the meeting, but the message – which was of course loud and clear, that we should return to blue – was to be relayed back to him. Mehmet Dalman, the Cardiff City chairman, spoke to the media about the meeting and things were sounding positive – the thing we had campaigned in favour of for so long might finally come about after all – Cardiff City might finally be going back to **BLUE!**

There was the question of whether we could play in blue in our very next game the following day, against Fulham. A side note in FA rules – which I myself had looked up some time ago, and I had even emailed the FA for further clarification at one point – states that for one game in the season, a club is allowed to change its colours. The hope was that in these exceptional circumstances, the FA would also allow the club to be returned to blue permanently for the rest of the season.

So, finally, it was simply a case of waiting to hear the verdict. The news was filtering through from around 12am, but by 2pm on Friday, January 9th, it was clear that Vincent Tan was agreeable to restoring the club's home kit and badge. In his statement he announced how his Buddhist mother had aided him in reaching his decision. The battle was over – victory for all those who had been campaigning had been achieved. Perhaps, particularly in light of Tan's statement at Christmas time just weeks before, it came as a bit of a surprise, but it did seem as if common sense was finally prevailing. At last, the day had come, and no doubt the parties would then commence on the day that might be forever known as Blue Friday.

Section 3:

The Sad Crew: The Untold Story of the Ordinary Cardiff City Fan

'I do believe that if you haven't learnt about sadness, you cannot appreciate happiness.'

NANA MOUSKOURI

Introduction

Following Cardiff City in the 90s was not like following them now. At that time, the club was known pretty much only for the reputation of its fans, in particular the hooligan element known as the Soul Crew. But what is often forgotten, or brushed under the carpet, is that there were also quite a number of ordinary fans who followed the club at the time. This section of the book aims to lift the lid and expose what it was like being among these ordinary fans.

In some ways, the term ordinary fan is not quite correct either. To be a fan of a club struggling at the bottom of the football league took some doing, and an element of lunacy, regardless of whether you chose to vent your frustrations by way of violence directed at opposing fans. And despite cloaking yourself in the 'ordinary' guise, many was the time that, due to being surrounded by some of the hooligan element, you had no choice but to up your game a bit, and put on a bit of a show of bravado. Whether this meant joining in with conversations about where and when potential 'trouble' was likely to arise, or perhaps joining in with chants encouraging rival fans to meet with us outside – it didn't mean that you had to actively participate.

One of the key points about supporting the club in those days was what was happening on the terraces; what people were singing, what people were wearing. The football itself really was of insufficient quality to merit it being the main topic of conversation. A conversation about Cardiff City these days revolves around the form of certain players, strategy, formation, etc. People seem to think that being able to discuss the team's players in detail proves how much they know. Back in the day, you knew most of the players, but you wouldn't spend hours talking about how great they were. It was more about how we were going to get to Leyton Orient next week, how we were going to save money for it, and who we could expect to see there.

One of the things about being an ordinary fan is that you're never really in touch with the club and the important people associated with it. You read about what goes on in the *Echo*, or these days, on the message boards and on facebook. You have no aspirations to really have anything to do with what goes on with the club. These days some people seem to think they can have more influence, and in many ways, they can – a simple post on a message board and if it catches on who knows where it might lead. But back then no ordinary fan had any such delusions of grandeur. The name Annis Abraham had a certain notoriety. I was always impressed that his name appeared in programmes as a sponsor of players when usually it would be the names of businesses rather than individuals. Annis was one of our most famous hooligans long before the BBC did a documentary on him and garnered respect for this alone. Bear in mind that the ordinary fan in those days was not always against football violence as they mostly seem to be now – it was accepted as part and parcel of football culture, even if you didn't take part yourself. But as an ordinary fan, you never imagined you would have any dealings with the club hierarchy. Even someone like Vince Alm, the chairman of the Cardiff City Supporters Club. I held him in a certain sense of reverence simply for his unfaltering commitment, but I couldn't pretend that he was really someone I knew or that I was anywhere near his circle of acquaintance. If I knew the name of the barman at the Ninian Park pub, I would consider that inside info.

As an ordinary fan, you knew your place, and that would be, for the most part, a pretty lowly place. But by no means was there any kind of exclusivity. The fan base was nowhere near big enough for this to occur. As long as you kept going to as many matches as you could, you'd find yourself being able to hold your own as a fan. And for me, the thing that kept me going back was a great feeling of camaraderie. Cardiff fans always sang their hearts out, win or lose, and it was always good being among that.

The Early Days

I'm not going to lie, I'm pretty sure the first football match I ever attended was at The Vetch, Swansea's old ground. How sad is that, coming from a Cardiff fan?!

Although I first started school in Cardiff, when I was about six, we moved to Bridgend, about halfway between Cardiff and Swansea. It's more of a rugby town really. In the 70s, when I was growing up there, Bridgend were one of the best rugby sides in Wales, and Wales was the best of the home nations, so of course, there was a certain amount of pride about the place. I mostly played rugby in school. I wasn't too bad, but started losing interest once I got into my mid-teens.

I would have been nine at that game at the Vetch. It was Swansea v Spurs. Swansea were in the old First Division after John Toshack, the manager at the time, had somehow achieved the feat of getting them there. My dad was a Spurs fan so it was a good game to go to. I seem to remember that the win for Swansea meant that for a short time at least they actually went top of the league, incredibly enough. The next season however, Swansea were relegated.

When I was in my mid-late teens, I saw sense and started going down to Ninian Park. Unfortunately though, I can't remember my very first Cardiff game! I started going with my older brother or maybe a school friend or two. I even took my girlfriend, Helen, to one or two games, and she tried to show some interest. My main passion at that time was music – I was madly into indie music. I listened to John Peel, bought the *NME*, bought my records from Spillers and my clothes from wherever I could find that had clothes that looked sort of indie. With my indie haircut I probably looked a bit out of place on the football terraces, but then again, sometimes on the Grange End there might be so few of us it was difficult to say who exactly was 'in place'.

As I got older it became clear that any money I spent was going to be largely divided between the two equal passions of music and football. When I went to university in Reading I met some other football fans, including the two Marks, one short, and one tall, who had not known each other before but became firm friends due to their equal love of West Ham. I also met Ian from Shrewsbury, an Aston Villa fan. We had been at the same table for the first dinner at the halls of residence we were staying at and had been the only two people who refused to stand up and sing 'God Save The Queen'! Particularly impressive for Ian, as he was in fact English of course, but both of us were taking an anti-Royal stance – or an anti-Royal remaining-seated, in this case.

I stayed with Ian in Shrewsbury once and was introduced to the concept of the English Border Front, something that I hadn't been aware of before. After going to the pub one evening, we encountered a guy who was a bit aggressive, and also, my car was stolen (my mum's Mini Metro in fact) while I was there, but these two incidents could easily have been entirely unrelated to the EBF! Fortunately the car did turn up, pretty much unscathed.

While at Reading I got referred to as the Welshman quite a lot, but it was all in good humour. After one particularly satisfying win which actually made the national papers – I think it might have been the win over Man City in the fourth round of the FA Cup – I posted the news clipping up on the door of my room for everyone to see.

One of my best friends from Bridgend, Steve, who was also a big football fan, also went to Reading. In one year Steve and

I both lived in the same shared house. It was a drab time of living off £2.99 bottles of wine (wiiiiine, as Steve referred to it) from the Co-op, Tesco Value Baked Beans (with added cheese, this became Beans on Toast Supreme, or simply, Supreme), watching the quiz show, *Fifteen to One*, on a TV in a tiny box room, and the occasional Snappy Tomato Pizza. We would also watch the Premiership games, especially on a Monday in the College Arms, or Jarms as Steve liked to call it. Steve will not like me for saying this, but he did sponge quite a bit of money off me for beer in those days (although he did pay a lot of this back in later years). I had parents I could call upon for money, but when even this option was not available, we resorted to trying our luck on fruit machines – there was one in town that seemed to pay out more frequently than others, and I think we actually thought at one time that this was going to be our route out of poverty!

The advantage with being in Reading was that it wasn't too far from London, and so a few times, Steve and I made our way across on the train for Cardiff games against the London teams also in the lower reaches of the league, such as Barnet and Leyton Orient. Even against a lowly team like Leyton Orient I can remember there being talk about how a load of Chelsea fans were coming down to meet the Cardiff lot. These things almost always turned out to be nothing more than rumours but it meant you were always on your guard, and it added a bit of excitement to the prospect of the afternoon's activities.

The one time I went to Barnet was a pretty miserable day out. I realised why it is that Barnet seems to so often be the butt of many football fans' jokes – it was not much more than a park pitch with an open terrace for away fans. What made it worse was that if we had won our last FA Cup tie, on that day, we would in fact have been playing Arsenal. And I'm absolutely certain that this was what a copper/comedian outside the ground was referring to when, as we were walking in, with drizzle compounding the misery, he said something about there being 'a big game at Arsenal today.' As I recall, a dour game ended in a 0-0 draw for Cardiff.

Another team that was quite close to Reading was Wycombe, and I went there a couple of times. Wycombe were newly promoted from the Conference. They had quite a nice ground despite it being small. We always seemed to lose to them by at least three goals, but my memories of the Cardiff away support at these games are among the best I have.

At one game, I remember the fans shouting the names of each player and then getting every single one of them to do the ayatollah before the start of the match. Maybe this was done a few times around that time but only at Wycombe did I see it done for every single player. Even now, throughout the match, three or four of our players will be encouraged to do the ayatollah, but for every single player to individually do the ayatollah before the start was something else.

And then, we literally sang from start to finish. We would be 3-0 down and still continue singing as if the scoreline was a secondary consideration. Of course, we still wanted Cardiff to win, but expectations were not as high back then. Cardiff at that time were unique in the way that we would continue singing, even immediately after the opposing side had scored. The other team would score and their fans would make a bit of noise for a couple of minutes and they would turn to us and just be amazed that we were still singing like nothing had happened. They certainly could not shout, 'You're not singing anymore!' at us, but of course, if we could be bothered to acknowledge their meagre output of noise, we could quite easily chant, 'You only sing when you're winning!' at them.

I think Wycombe actually picked up a few things from Cardiff. I heard them a few years later and instead of being quiet, they had become quite vocal, singing similar chants to the ones we used to chant.

We used to sing 'One Man Went to Mow', which was quite a good one for any rare gaps of silence because it was quite long and a little bit boring. By the end of it someone had usually thought up a much better chant that everyone would get into again.

Chants come and go, of course. These days, sadly, a lot of chants Cardiff sing are pretty much the same as the ones supporters of every other club sing. There's no denying Cardiff's support has got a little bit boring. Even when we're noisy now it can be a bit boring because it's always the same. Back in the day I'm sure there was more variety. There were also far more chants invented on the spur of the moment which hardly ever seems to happen now. These ones usually turn out to be some of the best.

While I was at university I also went to watch a friendly between Reading and Spurs at Reading's old ground, which was a little like Ninian Park. At that time I was probably only going to maybe six or seven games a season, but when I left Reading and moved back to Cardiff, I started going a lot more often as I started to become a more committed supporter.

Meeting Neil (If Found, Please Return to the Back of F Block)

It was hardly the place you might expect to find a Cardiff City fan. An old school friend of mine, Julian, who worked for Friends of the Earth, had organised a house party. He had house parties quite often at that time – around the mid-late 90s – and in fairness, they were always pretty good, with a good number of people, plenty of booze, maybe some weed. But they were mostly arty/hippy people, as you might expect – not too many football fans amongst them.

Neil happened to be at this party. He was a volunteer for Friends of the Earth at the time. We struck up a conversation and quickly discovered we had a mutual interest in Cardiff City and the conversation from that point forward was devoted pretty much to that one topic, along with our mutual interest in Welsh football in general.

Bear in mind, if this needs reiterating, that Cardiff City fans were a relatively rare breed at this time. People might have difficulty in understanding this, but back in those days if you were in town and saw someone wearing a Cardiff City shirt, you would feel compelled to stop and have a conversation about whether Kevin Nugent would ever recover his form or how Stant missed that sitter. These days, you pass someone in the street wearing Cardiff City clothing and barely acknowledge them with a smile or nod. If you shouted 'Bluebirds' or called for them to do the ayatollah they'd think you were nuts.

So anyway, two Cardiff City fans at a party having a conversation would not have been such a common thing as it might be today. We would have discussed the plight of the team, whether we would ever manage to stay up in the third division, instead of always yo-yoing between the third and fourth divisions; which players were showing at least a basic level of ability; which games we might possibly be expecting to get to ourselves. Seriously – no Cardiff City fan was expected to have a season ticket in those days – that really was an incredibly rare breed (filed under lunatic).

We agreed to meet up at a game. I'm fairly sure the first game I ever watched with Neil we had not met up before in the pub but had met inside the ground. Neil would go into the one section of Ninian Park that was actually pretty quiet for much of the time, the right side of the Bob Bank as you looked at the ground. Yet Neil was one of the loudest people in the whole stadium.

To say that Neil stood out like a sore thumb was somewhat of an understatement. He would sing at the top of his voice and join in noisily with the chants being sung at the other end of the Bob Bank. His passion could not be faulted, but being next to him in this quiet section, could be more than a little embarrassing.

Neil was eccentric, there was no doubt about that. He was enthusiastic and had an optimistic streak that would put any Monster Raving Loony candidate who ever dreamed of being elected to shame. Cardiff could be looking at mid-table mediocrity for yet another season but until the point at which it was mathematically impossible for it not to happen – usually around, say, 15 games before the end of the season – Neil would be apparently convinced that Cardiff were going up as champions and he would unwaveringly tell everybody this.

You couldn't fault him as a fan, but initially, my mate Steve and I were inclined to try and avoid Neil simply because his boisterousness could be a bit overwhelming. I also hated going in the quiet section of the ground, preferring the noisier section nearer the away fans. The problem was it was extremely difficult to get Neil to change his mind about anything. His favourite pint always was, and still is, Stella, for example, and if you can ever get him to drink Carling or Fosters, even when that's all that's on offer, you've done well indeed (as Fosters is the only lager on sale inside the new stadium he no longer has a pint at half-time). In spite of the fact that he clearly was not suited to this quiet section, getting him to move to somewhere where he might fit in proved to be a difficult task.

But at some stage we must have achieved this. I seem to remember he was slightly uncomfortable initially being amongst others who were also shouting their heads off. Perhaps because he liked to be the one who stood out. But once he settled into his new role of being among like-minded others, Neil moving to F Block proved to be not only a godsend, but a revelation!

There's a certain skill involved in getting a chant going, that is, getting a large number of people to join in with a chant that you've started. It might involve singing the very last part of a chant so that when you come to start the chant again from the beginning, everyone will then join in – that could be said to be the subtle method. Neil's method was anything but subtle. He would just shout at the top of his voice, like a general barking out orders, and the troops would feel compelled to join in.

The F Block already had a reputation for being probably the loudest section of the Bob Bank if not the whole of Ninian Park, even if it was not the cool hang-out of the serious hooligans. It didn't need someone to come along and try to take it over. But Neil's role in this section of the crowd cannot be understated. He helped boost the noise levels just that little bit further. There were times when he could be annoying and he knew that himself. But he would just stick to the task of keeping the volume up to the max.

If Neil got a chant of 'Barmy Army' going, it could go on probably for around 10 minutes. At times practically the whole of the Bob Bank would be singing and clapping along. It might fade to just one or two people, but Neil would carry on, still at the top of his voice. Some people around him would even become visibly disturbed by his tenacity, but then a few more people would join in again, then a few more, before once again, practically the whole crowd would continue the chant, and there was no room to feel uncomfortable.

Towards the later days at Ninian Park there was a pretty large contingent of regulars who we would see at the back of F Block, some of whom we knew the names of, others who would become known by their nicknames. There was a group of four or five guys who came up from Port Talbot and these guys got the maximum respect coming from a town just outside of Swansea. One of them was known simply as 'Opera' because when he started a chant of 'Ooooohhhh!!!' to get people to do the ayatollah, he sounded like an opera singer! There was Rob, a tall guy who always stood right at the very back – he drove us to a couple of away games, cracking fellow. Everybody knew Neil as Neil, but for a short time, he was known as Badger. This was because shortly after he met his girlfriend, who is now his wife, one morning, he woke up and half of his hair had gone white! I don't know if it was the shock of finally getting a girlfriend or it may have been some stress he'd had to deal with in work – he put it down to one of these two things, or both. The white did fade but the nickname stuck for a little while.

Neil had an old-fashioned sense of decency – he was always friendly with the stewards, and despite being loud, was polite most of the time. He might sometimes seem a bit stuck in the past – he's the sort of person who, even now, will still refer to Cardiff Bay as The Docks, despite the area having been redeveloped well over ten years ago. Neil had pretty good general knowledge and a good grasp of history but just did not seem to hold too much truck with modernity – the internet would become another thing that he would claim to have little understanding of, or need for (although he does claim to have got to grips with it now, which is helpful, as he has to use it in work).

Neil and I went to quite a few away games together. Neil would usually prefer to book up with the official Supporters Club, which personally I felt was a bit of a safe and conventional method of transport, but at least it was convenient. We would usually get picked up at Pentwyn, near to Neil's house.

For one away game versus Bristol we went on the train. In a packed carriage, we were literally the only ones who were not wearing Burberry/Aquascutum, which was de rigueur at the time. Neil had his replica shirt and cap on as usual. I'm not too sure what I was wearing but it definitely wasn't Burberry. If ever there was a stark picture of the contrast between the hooligan and the ordinary fan this was it. The irony for me was that we had managed to get on without tickets whereas the majority of the hooligan-types around us had apparently bought tickets (this was after barriers were introduced at Cardiff Central, but before they'd been installed by the lifts, so you could still go up to the platform in the lift and get on a train; so long as there weren't any barriers at the other end, you could often get away with it).

We were made to walk the couple of miles from Bristol Temple Meads to the ground by police escort, and typically, Neil spent most of the journey chatting in a friendly manner with the police without a care in the world for the supposed reason why we were being escorted. After the game we were made to march back to the station, again by the police. A couple of hundred at the front started chanting 'Soul Crew, Soul Crew!' Then the rest of us, around five hundred in the pack behind chanted, 'Bluebirds!' and 'Blue Army!' It really was like a military operation.

We finally went to a Wales away game in 2005, against Austria. This was all booked through Red Arrow travel. Neil had already been on a few international trips. I had been overseas once to watch Cardiff play some pre-season friendlies in Northern Ireland but this felt a lot more like a proper trip following a team abroad. Essentially it is one long piss-up. You can meet some real characters and many people who may become lifelong friends. We had our photos taken with the newly installed Wales manager John Toshack at the U21s match before the main game. Neil and I tried out all sorts of bars and had a cracking time. We even had a chance to see some of the local tourist attractions, such as the statue of Beethoven and the Belvedere Palace. We met some nice young ladies but, in the pre-facebook days, there wasn't much chance of us staying in touch long-term.

Neil was arrested once at an away game. This was at Coventry. My brother had driven up, and another friend, Nigel, had come too, so there were four of us altogether. We found a pub a little way from the ground and had a few beers there. We were in quite good spirits by the time we got to the ground. We took our place in the queue at the turnstiles but Nigel made the mistake of asking one of the police if we were definitely in the right queue. The next thing he was being arrested for being drunk. He was taken away without us immediately realising what had happened. Neil was furious. Inside he spent most of the first half berating the police, trying to find out where Nigel had been taken, and asking to speak to the most senior officer in charge. At half-time he carried on until the police got so tired of him that they arrested him and took him away as well. Fortunately both of them were released later that night but my brother and I had to make a couple of trips up to Coventry in case we were needed to speak on Neil's behalf. Eventually all charges against Neil and Nigel were dropped without a hearing ever even taking place. Neil's behaviour at the game was typical of him though – maybe it was silly of him to get himself arrested, but although he was no hooligan, Neil was not a person to be messed around, and he had an unwavering sense of loyalty to his friends.

Since Cardiff have moved to their new stadium I don't see as much of Neil. I didn't renew my season ticket for our first season there and as a result Neil got a seat on his own, in a quiet section, just like where he used to go when I first met him. I still see him sometimes before games and usually in the half-time interval, but my regular position in the stadium is on the other side of the stand to him. I think he feels a bit of sadness about this – I know a lot of fans were unsure where to go when we changed stadiums, but I guess I should at least have ensured I went near to Neil. In terms of regenerating the atmosphere I often think that moving Neil nearer to where I usually go – that is, closer to the away fans – would probably help in terms of getting people to sing again. That's how much of an influence he could be. But, once again, now he's found his regular spot, he's reluctant to change. And besides, he actually says he thinks his singing (as he calls it) days are over, and it's time for some young fans to step up to the plate. Maybe he's right but I still say he could show people how it's done again.

One final thing to reflect on – throughout the whole time that Neil kept telling us to keep the faith, even when we were lingering in the lower divisions, when it came to us finally going up through the leagues under Sam Hammam, it really did feel that Neil's unfaltering optimism was finally coming to fruition. He may have sounded mad back in the late 90s, but since then we've been promoted three times and been to Wembley for the FA Cup and Carling Cup finals. Who'd have thought it, but Neil was proven right.

Three Aways (Cambridge, Torquay and Blackpool)

There are a couple of away games that stick in my mind particularly. The first of these was Cambridge Utd in the 98/99 season. Steve and I had gone on a Supporters Club coach, leaving from Ninian Park, when Tony Jeffries was still running it. He had issued a fairly strict warning that anyone found with alcohol on the coach would be thrown off, so anyone who had any on them should leave it behind. This prompted Steve and I to disembark (so keen were we to not miss the trip) and hide our bottles of cider near to the ground, hoping we could pick them up on our return (some chance – the bottles were nowhere to be seen when we got back). Of course, this is in stark contrast to the coaches Tony runs now, which have a more relaxed policy, shall we say. But the Supporters Club has always sensibly stuck to the law.

The Supporters Club has always been more family-orientated, but at that time, even on the Supporters Club coaches, you would find that much of the discussion by people of all ages on the journey up, especially as the coach neared its final destination, would be about potential trouble, and the likelihood of the opposing fans being up for it. The whole mindset of the typical Cardiff fan really was quite a lot different in that time, but it was simply considered the norm.

According to reports, we took 2,200 fans to Cambridge that day – a considerable number for a team in the lowest league, but this was after all a mouth-watering top of the table clash. The game actually coincided with the Oxford/Cambridge boat race, but I don't suppose that the Cambridge fans – presumably by far the majority being local residents as opposed to students – had too much interest in this.

The most notable thing about this particular game was that, despite ending 0-0, it was a terrific game of football, and as the Cambridge manager observed afterwards, an excellent advert for lower-league football. Each side went at it hammer and tongs, with some real skill on display. The stats say that there were not that many attempts at goal but I recall it being real end-to-end stuff.

In addition, the game spawned perhaps one of the best spur of the moment chants I think I've ever heard. Bear in mind that these were the top two sides in the league and both teams were playing extremely well. Also bear in mind that the chant 'You're shit, and you know you are' was very popular at the time (although not quite so favoured by Cardiff as with some teams). And then bear in mind of course Cardiff's reputation as the club with some of the toughest fans. So taking all that into consideration, especially the fact that Cambridge were playing very well, someone must have considered it just not appropriate for us to sing, 'You're shit, and you know you are', and instead got us all to sing the more respectful, 'You're not very good, you're not very good…'!

It was just genius in my mind. I am almost 100% certain that this was the game where this chant was started. There could have been few games where this chant would have worked in the same way. However, it was used occasionally over the years, but in the wrong context. It started being used sometimes when the other side *really wasn't* very good! For example, at Sunderland away a few years later (another 0-0), after Sunderland had come down from the Premiership with, if I remember rightly, the lowest ever Premier League points tally, and were then also struggling in the Championship. It was even used by England fans at the Millennium Stadium in 2011, obviously many, many years after that Cambridge v Cardiff game, and so quite amusing to hear it in some ways, after somehow the English fans had picked up on it, but again, obviously, used in the wrong context (Wales *really weren't* very good!).

At the end of the game against Cambridge, I remember the sight of seven or eight large-looking lumps removing their shirts and singing songs in demonstration of their hatred of our West Walian rivals, while at the same time exposing several Cardiff and Wales tattoos. As a 20-something fan I was impressed again that anyone could be a sufficiently fervent supporter of this lower league club to get a tattoo done (I did in fact get my own Cardiff tattoo done a few years later, after we won promotion to the Championship via the play-offs).

As we made our way back to our coaches, some teenagers still had not had enough and were determined to find some Cambridge fans game for a fight. They could hardly have been upset by the result – a draw meant our promotion was still well on track, and it had been a great game, as mentioned – but nonetheless, the spirit of the time was, we must fight no matter what!

The 0-0 in the corresponding fixture the following season, both teams having won promotion, is the one that may be talked of more, despite there being just five hundred travelling fans for this midweek game at Christmas time. Cardiff were reduced to eight men and the goalkeeper, John Hallworth, a legend at that time – Cardiff have always had good keepers – saved a penalty right at the death (worth looking up the radio commentary by Phil Suarez on YouTube for this – hilarious), but nonetheless the one that I went to was still memorable as a cracking game of football.

In 2000, Steve and I went to Torquay because a friend from school was studying to be a doctor there. When you see just how some people behave, especially in respect of alcohol consumption, you have to question how they can be allowed into the medical profession, but that's a discussion for another time. For this trip, we had decided to go down on the train. Traditionally, the train has always been considered to be the hooligan's transport of choice, perhaps partly because there are zero restrictions on alcohol.

I remember that as we neared the main Torquay station most of the hooligan-looking lot got off at least one station before, presumably in the know about pubs in the area, or perhaps there was a pre-arranged 'meet'. Who knows, but Steve and I were not going to follow their example, and besides, we had our own meeting arranged with our friend Rich at Torquay. We also met another friend of ours, Paul, at the ground.

This game would be legendary for two reasons. First of all – Cardiff's comeback. We had trailed 1-0 at half time, but came back to win 4-1, including a hat-trick by Earnie. This inspired the second memorable moment when a chant was started to the tune of 'Who Let The Dogs Out?', a big hit at the time by the Baha Men (produced by Jonathan King – not a lot of people know that!). So the chant was 'Who Let The Goals In? Jones, Jones, Jones, Jones, Jones!' (Jones being the name of the Torquay keeper). This won't sound as good on paper, and yes, you had to be there. It's difficult to describe the moment when a genius on-the-spot chant breaks out, but a really good one can be quite special. The significance of this, along with a couple of other songs sung which I can't quite remember, was that the Torquay fans on the far side from us, in what could barely be described as a football ground, let alone a stadium, could clearly be seen to be in hysterics. Their side had just conceded a 1-0 lead, and were now facing a heavy defeat, but instead of looking glum, they were laughing at one of our chants – that's how good it was!

On this rare occasion – because we had somewhere to sleep (Rich's room in his hall of residence) – we stayed over. There was a bit of mayhem in one of Torquay's night spots, with some other of Cardiff's fans also there, including one guy who I think is referred to in the *Soul Crew* book as Scouser. I don't remember getting a particularly good night's sleep with the four of us crammed into Rich's little space.

Quite a few away games, especially when going on a Supporters coach, will be a simple bus journey up, into the ground, maybe a pint or two, watch the match, and back, but sometimes we would stay a bit longer. One of these was Blackpool away.

I think I must have gone to Blackpool twice back in the day, because one time I remember us being herded by police into the Manchester bar before the match, where we were entertained by strippers at 1pm! Nice of the police to decide that this was what we needed to calm any pre-match nerves. Anyway, I'm fairly sure this was a separate trip to the one I made around October time with Neil, Nigel and Steve.

On this trip, despite the fact that it was on a Supporters coach, they had extended the time before the bus was due to leave to allow us to sample the bars along Blackpool's seafront. Out of season, they were not much to write home about. I remember it being freezing cold as we battled against the wind, flitting from bar to bar. In one of them, I had an encounter with what I suspected to be Man Utd fans in the loo. I was pretty sure they were keen to inflict some form of injuries on me, mainly because of my Welsh accent

I was outnumbered, and was not really sure how I was going to get out of this one, but for some reason, in my drunken state, it occurred to me to ask them, 'Yes, but can you say Llanfairpwllgwyngyllgogerychwyrndrobwllllantysiliogogogoch?' This left them a bit flummoxed, and while they floundered for an answer to this ridiculous question, I made my escape. They had definitely been owned by The Sad Crew on this occasion.

We were back in time for the bus which must have been due to leave at around 10pm. One person was missing from the bus – Jock, a jovial Scot who, for some reason, had latched onto Cardiff City – I think it was because his missus was Welsh, hence his move down to south Wales. He must have eventually boarded, no doubt drunk as a skunk, because I'm certain I remember us chatting to Jock all the way back. Jock was the first person to introduce me to the expression 'Jackland' as a term for Swansea. Jock lived in Bridgend, so Swansea was a little closer for him, and he would talk of how he delighted in going out to the clubs in Jackland to cause a bit of bother before returning to his girlfriend in Bridgend.

I still see Jock at games today – he has aged a bit and appears to have mellowed a little in his old age. He is not permanently drunk, and this is partly because he quite often drives a coach to games himself now and apparently takes this responsibility seriously. One of the funniest sights I've seen was Jock at the Scotland v Wales game at Hampden Park in 2013 among the Wales fans with a Welsh flag draped around his shoulders. Clearly, he has taken his Bluebirds mentality to its logical extreme, even feeling the need to support Wales over his native land. You do meet some real characters along the way as a football fan, and Jock undoubtedly is one of them.

My Year As A Programme Seller

Just prior to the start of the 99/00 season, when I was twenty-seven, I applied for a job with Cardiff City which I'd seen advertised in the *Echo*. The job was something to do with marketing and promotions, which I didn't exactly have a great deal of experience in, but I thought I could give it a try.

I made it to the interview stage, which was to take place at the ground, and it was quite exciting getting to see some of the behind-the-scenes areas at Ninian Park. I got to see some of the trophy cabinets and lists of honours. I really had no expectations that I had any chance of getting this job. I had just finished a fairly dull job as a storeman, and wasn't sure about starting another full-time position straight away – I had an idea of setting up my own business instead.

The person who interviewed me seemed to think I was going to be suitable for the job. He actually said he was quite impressed by my application and that in fact, they'd had quite a large number of applications and I was among only a handful to reach this stage. Part of the problem for me though was that I really was not clear what the job entailed and exactly what my role would be. In my mind as well, I was more concerned about the business idea I had – I'd decided I was going to finally have a try at setting up a record label, which was something I'd always wanted to have a go at – and I thought that if I started the job at Cardiff City I wouldn't have the time to devote to my business.

So in spite of the fact that the interviewer was practically telling me that I could have the job, I declined it, but as they had also been advertising for programme sellers I said that I would do this instead. I have to say that this is one of the biggest regrets of my life. I'm sure I'd have picked it up once I'd got started. When would I ever get the chance again to get a good job with the football club I loved? In spite of the fact that I couldn't play football I seem to remember that I also had a ridiculous dream at the time of being a player for the club! If I'd just had the sense to realise that this was an impossible dream and that instead here was a chance for a real opportunity, I might actually have gone on to have a successful career with Cardiff City. Inevitably my own business idea never properly got off the ground.

So at the start of the 99/00 season I found myself reporting to the office to pick up programmes to sell. Actually, I say this, but I know that for the very first game of the season I was in town to see the arrival of the visiting Millwall fans who took over a chunk of Mill Lane (appropriately enough), so perhaps I didn't start until maybe the second or third game.

There wasn't a great deal to it, as you might imagine. You had a great big bag of the things and would stand in one of the designated spots and, well, sell programmes. I would start around two hours before kick-off and it was always quiet to begin with. As it got closer to kick-off you'd be selling them with a greater degree of frequency. By ten to three there was a relative frenzy of activity as things reached fever pitch with the public's demand for programmes reaching almost unprecedented levels of near hysteria...

At least I would get to see the players arriving. I would see the likes of Kevin Nugent, Richard Carpenter, etc. and make the occasional comment on their last performance or give a few words of encouragement for the forthcoming match. There were always a few fans who would hang around to also greet the players. One of these included Dai Hunt, who is a bit of a legend amongst City fans. He is mostly considered a tad on the annoying side, and Dai must know this but he really does not seem to care; instead he just continues being Dai Hunt, loud of mouth and blue and white of hat and scarf, always with the same unbridled enthusiasm. Let's be honest, at that time, Cardiff needed enthusiastic supporters, because without them there may have been a feeling of no hope whatsoever!

I got to meet a few other fans, and there were a few people who would regularly buy programmes from me. One of these was a girl called Lisa. She and her mum and dad were season ticket holders, at a time when season ticket holders at Cardiff were quite untypical, and they would even travel down from Birmingham for every home game. Lisa was blonde and quite attractive and was always friendly. I don't think she had a boyfriend at that time, and I think I imagined we might start up some kind of relationship – let's face it, it's probably every football fan's dream to meet a woman also genuinely into football. I did get her number at one point and at least once I sat with her and her mum and dad when Neil, who I usually went with, couldn't make it. But anyway, I suppose the distance was always going to be a problem, and it never quite happened somehow.

I actually had a season ticket myself for this season. Along with a small amount of pay, as a programme seller, you were also entitled to a free seat in the Grandstand, but as my friends all went in the Bob Bank I wanted to keep going there instead. As luck would have it, a couple of games into the season I met someone in the Admiral Napier who was selling his season ticket as he was moving abroad. He wanted £50 for it which I knew was a bargain price, but was still more than I could afford. I asked if he could hang on to it for me and I asked my dad if he could help me out in buying it. A few days later, I bought it, and I had my first ever season ticket for Cardiff City. It took the form of a blue plastic wallet with the club badge on it, and contained paper tickets for every match of the season.

I can't emphasise enough how uncommon it was for people to have season tickets at that time. We were lingering at the bottom of the lowest tier in the football league with attendances of not more than five or six thousand. The typical price per match was around £6, which you could just pay at the turnstiles. Of course, most of the fans going to watch Cardiff at that time would want to go to as many games as possible, but when you were so often seeing poor performances and poor results, being committed enough to want to witness every single one of these spectacles was not expected. There was even a scheme in one season where the price went up or down a pound or two depending on the result of the previous match!

In the end, I only lasted one season as a programme seller. I did actually quite enjoy it in a way and I felt like I was doing my little bit to help out the club. As well as meeting some of the fans I also got to meet the other programme sellers, who were all pretty passionate fans as well of course, and also got to meet the people who ran the club shop. I can't say it was all that memorable a time, but one occasion sticks in my mind. Cardiff had a visit from our friends across the bridge – Bristol City. We had quite a few programmes left over and it occurred to me that several of the Bristol fans, especially those who'd arrived late, might want a programme. I volunteered to go into the Bristol end and sell programmes. I felt like a cat in a dog pound as I walked cautiously along the front of the Grange End where the Bristol fans were being housed. 'Programmes!' I shouted out in my least authentically Cardiff accent. I had a PVC jacket to at least give me some kind of cover – this mob would surely not attack a staff member. Fortunately most of them did not seem to pay too much heed to me. One or two of them, almost out of respect for my quite apparent bravery it felt to me, did scurry down the aisle to take one of my wares. I did a quick up and down the stand before I returned to the safety of the programmes HQ.

Midway through this season I'd moved to live in a flat in Bridgend, which meant that getting to each game was proving more difficult and more expensive. So at the end of the 99/00 season my part-time profession as programme seller was at an end, but for Cardiff City, big changes were afoot and a whole new era beckoned.

Sam Hammam, My Lord, Sam Hammam

I don't care what anyone says, in my mind Sam Hammam was a genius and an inspiration. He may have left the club in debt but the five or so years supporting Cardiff City under his reign were for me by far the most exciting and entertaining. This was a man who had a true understanding of the club's fans. In the days of clubs having owners who apparently have nothing more on their minds than making money, and carrying out their business in a safe, corporate and conventional manner, here was a man whose ideas about how the club should operate were sometimes so controversial he was even more extreme than the fans he represented.

I was on the pre-season tour of Northern Ireland at the time the news was breaking that Sam Hammam would be taking over. The expectation that this would prove to be a good thing for the club was high. People had witnessed how he'd taken Wimbledon from obscurity and got them into the Premiership as well as winning the FA Cup. There may have been some apprehension regarding how things had ended up, but if he could get us a couple of promotions we weren't going to grumble.

We were indeed promoted in the first season with Sam Hammam in charge. What I liked about Sam was that he was a man with a clear vision. He would think about what he wanted to achieve and then set about achieving it. One of his biggest ambitions was to restore pride to the club. For a long time Cardiff had been considered a sleeping giant due to the fact that we had a large catchment area of fans, yet lingered in a lowly league position.

Sam felt that one way to get people back into supporting Cardiff City was to have a recruitment policy that positively welcomed more Welsh players. In this first season, then, we had Scott Young, Rhys Weston, Earnie, Danny Gabbidon and James Collins (these last two forging a quite formidable defensive partnership), as well as more seasoned players like Andy Legg and Jason Bowen. There was also a young player from Cardiff named Nicky Fish, who I'd always hoped would do well, being my almost-namesake, but tragically, he was involved in a severe road accident. A quick google tells me that after six years of being unable to play, he has most recently been playing for the Cardiff team, Bridgend Street.

It could be said that none of these players, except perhaps Earnie, could be considered exceptional talents, but they were all strong, useful and effective. All of these players also played in the Welsh national side, which meant that Cardiff fans could go to watch the Wales team and see a side that, to a large extent, was selected from the Cardiff team. This meant that the buzz at both Cardiff and Wales games was stronger than ever before. The numbers of people flocking to watch Wales was staggering, culminating in a 70,000-plus crowd, packing out the Millennium Stadium for the play-off game versus Russia in 2004 (Earnie's omission from the starting line-up is still talked about today).

To further instil this sense of pride, the song used in the film *Zulu*, 'Men of Harlech', which was popular with fans, was played over the tannoy system. Sam Hammam looked to change the club badge, but instead of thinking immediately of the Welsh dragon, Sam looked further afield. It occurred to him to use the St David's cross (used to represent the town of St David). People may not believe this now, as these days you see this cross everywhere, but genuinely, a little over ten years ago, this flag was hardly known about – Sam Hammam took it from obscurity and put it on the Cardiff City crest, which was genius in my eyes, because I thought this black and yellow cross, forming the background to the new badge, with the bluebird still prominently in front, looked great.

The new badge was a modern, simple and effective design. Some people said it looked like Leeds Utd's badge – well so what? Just about every badge will be reminiscent in some ways of other badges. It had the element that was most important to fans – the bluebird – at its core, with the strong Welsh element being represented by the St David's cross. This badge was also symbolic of success of course, as it was used throughout the time that Cardiff were doing well under Sam Hammam. In the 2008/2009 season, the old badge was brought in again, supposedly for just one season due to it being an anniversary year for Cardiff, but at the end of the year, it was apparently decided to keep the old badge on, which was a mistake in my opinion. The old badge had far more support, but to my mind this badge looked old-fashioned, and was more representative of the old and unsuccessful Cardiff City.

Sam had also talked of changing the club kit from blue to red, white and green but, just as he had listened to fans and made sure that the bluebird was kept central as part of the club badge, he also listened to fans and decided to keep the home kit as blue.

Sam did things for the Cardiff fans. At one game he presented everyone with a leaflet, like a mini-programme which outlined his personal objectives for the club, described as his own five year plan. He wrote in such an outlandish and enthusiastic manner that, quite frankly, a lot of people thought he was bonkers, but at the same time, people loved him for it. Here was someone who had come along and was showing an overwhelming passion for the club that, yes, we also loved, but for a lot of us, it had become like a marriage that was on the rocks. Yes, we still loved Cardiff, but we'd got a bit tired of the fact that it never quite satisfied us. Sam was like a sex therapist, geeing up our relationship with the club, and making us both feel good about ourselves.

Conditions at Ninian Park were improved – nothing major; we were promised after all that, in time, work would start on a new stadium – but there were new bar and toilet facilities. Reading the *Echo* became exciting (a miracle in itself), and people would look forward to reading Sam's latest crazy idea. For so long, Cardiff fans had grown tired of seeing people walking around Cardiff in the shirts of Man Utd, Liverpool, etc. To combat this Sam introduced a policy encouraging those people to bring in their shirts of other clubs and trade them in for a half-price Cardiff City shirt. Again, a simple idea, the sort of thing a fan might propose, but just genius coming from the club's owner. And Sam even proposed that all these shirts of other clubs should be put on a bonfire and burned. It was decided that this was taking things too far – but again, a perfect example of Sam having even more extreme views than the fans.

Sam tried to tackle the club's hooligan issue. But instead of keeping quiet and pretending it didn't exist, Sam spoke about the issue quite openly. In fact, more than that, he met with several of the club's known hooligans, and at one time even organised a bus for them all to travel to a game at his expense. It was uncertain exactly what the purpose of this was, and the act was widely criticised in the media and by people who were against hooligans. I suppose it was Sam's attempt at rehabilitation if that's the right expression, and I actually think it might have worked to some extent – he was aiding fans who had previously been alienated by the club's hierarchy and instead gave them the chance to be a part of what he was trying to achieve, which was to get one big unified fan base.

In the 01/02 season – Sam's second season in charge – two 'glamour' signings were made in Graham Kavanagh and Peter Thorne. I would argue again that these were still not exceptional talents, but they were easily good enough to encourage fans to think that the club was continuing to be ambitious, and had another promotion in its sights.

We did not win promotion that season, but the following season, we made the Championship play-off final. This would normally have been held in Wembley of course, but as the new Wembley was at that time in the process of being built, the Millennium Stadium in Cardiff was being used instead to host events of this kind. How perfect in that case that Cardiff should both make it to and then host the final which they would go on to win? To mark this occasion Sam had proposed that Cardiff fans should march from Ninian Park to the Millennium Stadium, and that he would lead the march on the back of an elephant! The elephant thing was decided to be just a little too over-the-top but the march certainly did still happen and that was great fun, really helping in terms of getting the fans worked up for the occasion, which frankly was one of the best days of my life.

One season, a limited-edition watch with the old Cardiff crest was brought out which my Gran got me as a Christmas present. It came with a certificate featuring Sam's printed signature, which I loved at the time. I must have had the watch for around ten years, wearing it every day without ever a thought for replacing it. Every year or two I'd have the battery replaced at Cardiff Central Market. Sadly, quite recently, first the glass broke, and then I somehow managed to lose it which was a bit of a heartache.

As I had read that Sam liked poetry, at one time I sent a book of my poetry to Sam via the club, and got a letter back, this time with Sam's genuine signature (featuring a large smiley symbol), with just the word 'Thanks!' printed in something like a 72-point font.

I met Sam only once, bumping into him in town, by chance, after a Wales match. I asked him a little about the game and talked about the number of Cardiff players in the side. Sam spoke with the same fevered excitement that you imagined from the tone of articles in the *Echo*. It was said that at that time Sam did not have a house in Cardiff, but instead often stayed in hotels in the city centre. I had bumped into him near the Angel Hotel, so perhaps that's where he was spending the night.

There were a couple of chants in recognition of Sam's achievements. The simple 'Sam Hammam, My Lord, Sam Hammam' became popular, and people would bow down to where Sam was seated in the stadium, or to where he was on one of his infamous walks around the pitch. It seems bizarre now that fans should do this, but it really was in recognition of unbounded support. Following the Leeds game – one of Cardiff's greatest triumphs, documented in much detail elsewhere – where Sam had been criticised for his walkabouts, the slightly ridiculous, 'We Want Sam Hammam Walking Round the Pitch!' chant started up.

Sadly, the wheels of the Sam Hammam bus finally started coming off around 2005. Sam's extravagances, it appeared, had led the club into financial trouble. They began by selling off players – Graham Kavanagh, our captain, was sold inexplicably, which actually led me to take a small banner to the back of the Bob Bank which read 'What the Fuck Is Going On?' I put it up on the back wall, and then strangely enough the Grange End started chanting this exact phrase in the second half – I can't believe they'd have been able to see my banner from all the way over there – perhaps it was just a coincidence that this phrase was pretty much how all of us fans felt.

As an ordinary fan I always feel that I never really have a full understanding of backstage goings-on. And really, it seems to me that Sam Hammam could only be criticised for what went on behind the scenes towards the end of his tenure and, admittedly, for some years after due to the seemingly forever overhanging debt. But in terms of onstage entertainment, for five years Sam and the players signed during his reign provided fans with a veritable feast – we could have asked for no more.

The Nightclub Years With Nigel and Blakey

Neil had two friends he'd known since school who, for a couple of seasons, would join us on the terraces. The first of these was Nigel, a very likeable character, who I sometimes think of as looking a bit like Harry Redknapp. Sometimes his downturned mouth looked a bit droopy, but then again he could smile and light up the room. The other was Blakey. Blakey was a big guy who would always wear a trench coat. He looked the hardest of all of us and would actually talk about the Soul Crew, although there was no direct evidence that he had anything to do with them. Blakey was blind in one eye following an accident when he was younger and seemed to always feel the need to tell people in advance about this on first meeting them – to put them at ease I suppose – but I honestly never noticed it, and to this day I don't know which eye it is.

A game that both Nigel and Blakey were coming to was undoubtedly a big one – maybe something like Brentford. We would often meet in The Westgate first for a game of pool and a pint. Nigel had a bit of a thing for fruit machines. In fact for almost the entire time – pre and post-match – Nigel would be on the bandits, and wouldn't talk to us much. He did seem to do incredibly well though – he nearly always seemed to win on them. There was one time, however, when he'd lost, and he'd asked to borrow a tenner off me to carry on. A tenner ten or fifteen years ago was obviously worth a bit more than it is now and I was a little reluctant. He swore that I would get it back as soon as we got into town. I said, in that case, why didn't he just go into town himself and get it out from a cashpoint? Well, he needed to carry on right now – probably, he thought there was a chance of the feature coming up or something. I stood my ground – I really did not want to be giving my friend more money just to keep on gambling. Nigel was furious with me! However, a short time after, once he'd been home and cooled down and perhaps discussed it with his girlfriend (and now wife), Donna, he actually thanked me! I don't think for a second I might have helped cure Nigel of any potential gambling problem (these days, I've got the habit myself, with my obsession with poker), but just at that moment I felt that I was doing the right thing. Also, of course, I'm a tight bastard, not willing to just dish out tenners willy-nilly.

One of my memories of Blakey was when we both worked at the AA Call Centre. Neither of us really liked it there – perhaps nobody did. Blakey had previously worked in a steelworks so this kind of work was not really his type of thing. I just couldn't stand the monotony of it, although some of the people I worked with were quite nice. On my very first day my assistant manager, Ceri, who was also a Cardiff fan, asked jokingly, 'Are you in the Soul Crew?' and I replied, also jokingly, 'No, I'm in the Sad Crew,' and this kind of stuck in a way.

Blakey's girlfriend at the time, Louise, for some reason liked to hang out on the gay scene. I think it was because her brother, Leon, was gay. So anyway, once or twice I did go with them to a couple of the gay clubs, despite it not really being my cup of tea. This one time, the club we went to had a night for gay football fans, and people were dressed in their football shirts for the occasion. This was completely unbeknown to us – we had just gone there by chance that night. It was a Friday, and the AA, like most call centres, had a dress-down Friday where you could wear what you liked instead of having to wear a formal shirt and trousers. Blakey had worn his Cardiff City shirt to work! Therefore, by a complete coincidence, he was then suitably dressed when we were later in the nightclub!

The club we did like going to was The Emporium. A full day's session would involve meeting at The Westgate or The Gatekeeper for a couple of pints at around 1.30pm before moving on to The Nin (the Ninian Park pub), where there might be time for either one more pint or perhaps a short.

It's good to have traditions and routines when going to the football – I'm sure every football fan does or should do. The phrase we would always reiterate was 'They never kick off without us.' It was Steve who particularly enjoyed the use of this expression. It might be five minutes to three in The Nin – a good five minutes walk from the ground itself – and one of us would still have at least half a pint to finish, but still we would always say, as one, 'They never kick off without us!'

Then we'd go to the match and usually have a beer at half-time before going back to The Westgate (possibly taking in The Nin again en route). From here, we would head into town. Quite often we'd go to The Model Inn next to The City Arms. The Model was known as a kind of pre-club pub. So we'd sink a few in here, getting a bit rowdy by this stage. There would usually be a few ladies about. Finally, by around 11pm, we would hit The Emporium. Drinks were a bit more expensive in here, although we would quite often indulge in double vodka-redbulls, which ten years or so ago, for no particular reason, were the in thing. Nigel might also have some speed or possibly even some Es, and we might have some and then just dance and get off our faces until about 4am.

The music in The Emporium was mainly house, and

although it was way past the heady days of raves and acid house, nightclubs in the late 90s/early 00s were still big business and house music was showing no signs of dying out. Time Flies – a club night that started in Cardiff in the mid-90s, and in fact is still going now, having recently celebrated its 20th anniversary – would often be held at The Emporium, and those nights were especially looked forward to.

Dancing was not easy when you'd been on the beer all day, but it could still be done with a couple of hours of slowing down a bit plus some extra chemicals inside you. You would see some absolute stunners in The Emporium who we'd chat to occasionally and, on very rare occasions, swap numbers. No facebook in those days of course, so if you really wanted to see someone again, you absolutely had to get their number, and this wasn't always easy – in the days of pre-mobiles (yes, those days did exist), you even had to go to the bar to get a pen, and the effort involved with this was off-putting for some people. Then again, because of the extra effort, for anyone to allow you to do this for them, it did mean it was more likely that they were genuinely interested.

The only thing with house music is that dancing to it usually involves virtually no contact. You could sometimes sort of sidle behind someone, but judging whether they were going to be into this or not was extremely difficult. One friend would try the gentle hand on waist approach first, and if he was rebuffed (this was 9 times out of 10), he would back off. It might sound a bit pervy but really, in the context of the loud music, the dark room, the lights, the stunning women, plus alcohol and drugs mixed in, it's surely understandable that everyone's state of arousal was at a premium.

There was one game when, for Steve and Neil's birthdays (both in December), we made a special booking with the club, which meant we had a pre-match meal, good seats in the Grandstand and we got to meet two of the players. The game was against Colchester – Steve, his brother Ben, Neil, Nigel, Blakey and I all went along. We were all dressed in suits and, for at least one match, we thought we were the business. I remember the meal being pretty good. We were all in good spirits. We had each chipped in to put a bet on Earnie scoring the first goal – this was the season when he broke the club record for goals scored in a season, so it was a pretty safe bet, and sure enough, that came in, which paid for our drinks for the day, at least.

We'd been put in the Grandstand, but for some reason – I can't quite remember why; probably Neil being a bit too noisy – we were asked to move at half-time. We were put in the front section, at the end of the Grandstand, next to the away fans. This section had the reputation of including Cardiff's most notorious hooligans. As we were all in suits, we actually experienced a lot of heads turning looking at *us*, wondering who the hell we were.

To top the day off, we met Earnie and the captain, Kav, who were both nice chaps, and we had our photos taken with them. That really was one of the best and most memorable days in the time I've supported Cardiff. It was a successful time for the club, and it was a great chance for a small group of fans, all close friends, to get together and enjoy ourselves.

When Cardiff won promotion to the 3rd division via the play-offs, we all watched the away leg of the play-off semi-final at Nigel's house. I remember Louise saying that Earnie looked like a Ferengie!

The play-off final, held at the Millennium Stadium, was another memorable day out. Again, the whole day was well choreographed. We started at a cafe on Caroline Street for breakfast. Don't remember too much of the day then to be honest, but I know that Steve and I ended up in Kiwi's (when it was still in the Wyndham Arcade) where Steve met Leon Fortune-West, and also managed to pull. At that time, I was living in a shared house in Roath. Steve and I, plus the girl he'd pulled, went back to the house, and stayed up for a while.

The boyfriend of one of the girls who lived in the house objected to us making a noise though, in spite of the fact that the next day was a bank holiday and Cardiff City had, after all, just won promotion to the Championship. He asked me to keep it down but we carried on a little while longer, and because of this, he came out of the room he was sharing, grabbed me, and punched me in the face. Unbelievable – and this bloke was studying to become a copper. I should also add that he was a rugby fan, so maybe another reason for being a killjoy.

I don't see Nigel or Blakey nearly as much these days – Nigel has settled down and has three kids, and Blakey has kind of drifted off in a way, but both of them are people that I know I could call on for just about anything at any stage in my life. We have had our differences and one or two things have happened that we might regret, but still, it's nice to know that football is one of the main things that has meant we have stayed together as friends.

Scary Moments

Being a 'normal' Cardiff City fan is probably quite a lot unlike being a normal fan of most other clubs. Even if you don't actively partake in violence, or don't seek it out, due to the fact that many others do (or did), the chances are that you're going to be caught up in things at one time or another.

In my case, this seemed to happen more often when I'd travelled to games on my own. In most cases, there was nearly always someone willing to travel to a game with me. I think it's different being a football fan to a music fan for example. If you're a music fan, you may have friends who also like music, but won't always want to go to the same gigs, whereas fans of the same football club are obviously always likely to want to travel to the same games. I didn't exactly travel with a mob but I usually knew one or two people who would be up for going to a game.

I did however travel up alone on a Supporters coach to Stoke away in 2000. I was keen to see this one as our survival in what was then Division Two rested largely on this result. We got to the ground, and I didn't particularly sense that this might be a trouble fixture. I think there may have been some history between Stoke and Cardiff which I was unaware of.

Cardiff went behind and our supporters were getting pretty agitated. The police had put up some tape to seal off the section at the front of the stand, but some fans broke through this, and were threatening to invade the pitch. Something overcame me and I felt that I needed to be among this lot, so I went to join them. I think some fans started ripping up a few seats. At one point, Andy Legg went to take a corner right in front of us, and I couldn't believe he was smiling as if nothing was going on. I didn't really know what to do myself, so I then left this section, and made my way towards the back of the stand again. After the match, with Cardiff having lost and relegation almost a certainty, was when the real trouble broke out.

I have to say, I did not actually witness this myself. As people left, again, I felt that I should be among the mob that was seeking trouble, and I went to join one lad who was heading towards where the police and the opposing fans were. He started shouting 'Soul Crew, Soul Crew!' and this was actually the first time I had ever heard these words used in the form of something like a battle cry. In those days, hooliganism was really a lot more serious, and the Soul Crew was generally a thing that was more undercover, and not spoken about except in perhaps more hushed tones (this changed, to some extent, after Tony Rivers' book came out, speaking more openly on the subject). So anyway, I suddenly felt as if I was amongst it, and I'm not going to lie, it scared me, so again, I backed out.

I went back to the bus, and felt like a bit of a wuss to tell the truth, as I was first to get on! The violence that followed is reported to have been amongst the worst Cardiff fans have been involved in. Some time later, the front cover of the *Echo* featured a rogues' gallery of faces the police were looking for in connection with this incident, and several arrests were made. As the chant goes, 'We're the best behaved supporters in the land... when we win! (But we're a right bunch of bastards when we lose).' To be quite honest, Cardiff could be just as bad when we won sometimes. Anyway, when I got back from that game, despite not having actually seen the worst of it, I told my parents, who I was living with at the time that I would never go to an away match again – just being amongst the hostile crowd had been enough to put me off. I didn't quite stick to this, however.

Tottenham away was another one. I had a friend of a friend who lived near to the ground, so I thought I would go to the match and stay with them at the same time. I seem to remember Neil and Nigel did also go to this game, but we had tickets for separate parts of the ground, which were sectioned off, so we couldn't meet up as arranged. It was an extremely cold night – there was even some snow. Cardiff did ok, though they weren't quite the match for Spurs, but it was a Cup game, so didn't really matter, and we weren't exactly expected to achieve all that much.

This game was not marred by violence, but it sticks in many people's memories due to the fact that the police made people walk through a nearby park in darkness. The person I was staying with lived just a couple of streets from the ground, but I, along with everyone else, had to go some distance out of my way. There were a lot of people wandering around the park, with no police in sight now, and nobody had any idea who was who. I remember I just kept my mouth shut and walked on, and then, once out of the park, I just kept going in silence. I think I walked for around four miles, before finally plucking up the courage to ask someone who did not look like a football fan, if they knew the street I was looking for, and fortunately, I was by now quite close, and found the house within minutes. People might scoff at this now, but back in the day, you really did have to be careful if you wanted to avoid a shoeing.

On another occasion I'd gone up to Wrexham for one of the FAW Premier games. I think they were actually holding the final up there that year. I was making the trip by train, again, on my tod. We had to change at Shrewsbury, and here, I met a group of about five young Cardiff fans, all drinking cider. They were quite a good group of lads, not exactly hooligans, but game for whatever came their way – there were a lot of fans at that time like that. I latched onto the group. We had a quick scout around Wrexham town centre first of all, going in the bookies, scaring a few of the locals. I think they were doing drugs as well, this lot. One of them somehow managed to get himself arrested before the start. We were just walking towards the ground, and he had a spliff, and the copper just came up and nicked him. Or maybe he'd tried to punch the copper. I can't quite remember, I just remember, it was a pretty needless arrest on his part. Well, we were one man down, but we still went to the match, his mates resolving to try and fetch him again afterwards.

The match was a pretty mundane affair. Afterwards, the Wrexham fans were leaving the ground at the same time as the Cardiff fans. The police presence was quite low, as I don't think any serious trouble was anticipated. But as we were walking away, one of this group was near to a Wrexham fan, and he just said to him something like, 'Are you a Wrexham fan?' to which the bloke just said yes, and the next thing, he jabbed him one on the nose! It was just pointless, but almost funny in a way – it wasn't exactly serious violence, just stupid really.

On the journey back, for most of the way, I was talking to a guy called Gary, who I would bump into from time to time at matches. Gary was a really big music fan, and was particularly into New Order. He was a little bit older than me. For just about any band you could name, Gary seemed to have a story about having seen them when they first started, when there were about twenty people there. He didn't boast about it, he would just tell me in a matter of fact sort of way.

Someone like Gary would be the sort of person that these days, when you got home, you would just add them on facebook, and instantly, you'd know about everything about them. Pre-facebook, there was more of an air of mystery. Who was this strange person that I would occasionally bump into on the train? When would be the next time I would see him, who knows?

I sometimes liked to think of Ninian Park as being the safest place on Earth – that was so long as you were a Cardiff fan. Being one amongst a large number of people who were all on the same side as you could be comforting, but Ninian Park was known for being one of the most intimidating grounds for away fans. Although I regularly went in the Bob Bank, for a change, I sometimes went in the Grange End, and here were the spikiest fans. Throughout the Sam Hammam era, home and away fans in the Grange End were separated by a variety of different forms of fencing, which seemed to vary depending on how recently more serious trouble had broken out. It was alongside the fence, closest to the away fans, that some of our most vociferous fans would hurl abuse over the partition. A lot of these people were in fact not even eighteen, and the things you would hear really could be pretty disgusting – enough to put the foulest mouthed soldier to shame. Not only was there the constant threat of 'sticks and stones', but the words were hurtful enough to make a mockery of that old rhyme. Just in complete contrast to the lines of silent supporters that line up near to the away fans at the new Cardiff stadium.

There was a time that, as you left Ninian Park, you had the option of going to the right, away from the ground, or turning to the left, towards the police and the away fans as they were coming out. There was certainly peer pressure encouraging people to make the left turn. For a time, this would honestly happen at just about every home game, regardless of the result. There would be a bit of a stand-off, a few things thrown. It really was simply part and parcel with the way things were at the time. It even got to the stage where at one time, we had gone to The Nin after the game, and the police were so concerned that our fans were going to get out and at the away fans that they actually surrounded the pub. It was strange given that the pub was a good few hundred yards away from the ground itself and pretty much in firm Cardiff territory. That only ever happened once to my knowledge, and that would have been in the mid-00s I think, but it just goes to show that despite what people say about the worst hooliganism being in the 70s and 80s, it was still an issue right through the 90s and into the 00s. For Cardiff it has only really died down since we have moved to the new stadium, and now things could hardly be more different.

I think other than a new type of fan coming in, and various changes and upheavals at the club, the main factors that I think have meant a diminishing amount of hooliganism at both home and away games for Cardiff are, first of all, the insanely heavy policing, and secondly, an increased number of cameras, meaning that the likelihood of getting caught and later sentenced are far higher. If there was ever a battle between police and fans, the police inevitably won mainly by sheer force of numbers. I remember going to QPR and just being overwhelmed by the number of police – it felt at times like there was something like one copper for every two fans. You would be made to walk through huge corridors of police, making you wary of even flinching for fear of being arrested for stepping out of line. It just got ridiculous, and the whole performance wore fans down in the end, I think, coupled with a high likelihood of a heavy sentence due to the greater surveillance.

As I've said, I was never involved in any violence, but hooligan or not, Cardiff fans stuck together. Unlike today, when at times it seems like fans are more divided.

I Didn't Predict a Riot

Towards the end of 1995, I was involved in an incident that has now become part of Cardiff City folklore, as well as being something still talked about by fans of The Stone Roses. At this stage, I had only been a Cardiff fan for around five or six years, and this was a few years before I met Neil, Nigel and Blakey.

As already mentioned, I was a big music fan in my teens, and was especially a fan of indie music. The band that really stood out for me was The Stone Roses, and this was a band that many people took to their hearts – I met one of my first true loves in the year that their debut album came out, so I'm sure that helped. Music and football did not necessarily mix all that much at that time, but The Stone Roses, along with some of the other Manchester bands of the time, did attract a following from hooligans and ordinary fans alike, perhaps people who in some parts would refer to themselves as scallies.

But anyway, in spite of the fact that I'd always been a big music fan, while I was at university in Reading, and I'd been going to a few away games, I think I'd made my mind up that I was now a bigger fan of Cardiff City than I was of The Stone Roses. I mean, that's not to say I wasn't still a borderline obsessive Roses fan. When their comeback single, 'Love Spreads', came out, I had a Love Spreads t-shirt, which I remember wearing to a club night at the university, in the hope that it might attract the attention of a girl called Zoe who I fancied the pants off there – I think Zoe was from Newport, and this t-shirt had the Newport crest on.

But anyway, The Stone Roses did not tour the *Second*

Coming album in Britain, released at the end of 1994, until the end of 1995. Give people a chance to learn the words, I suppose! The first date of the tour was in Cambridge, which wasn't too far from Reading, so I got a train across, and went to try and get into this gig, despite not having a ticket. Touts were selling tickets for around £50, which was outside of my price range, so I tried to blag my way in on the guestlist, to no avail. I actually claimed to be a reporter for the *South Wales Echo* (not sure why this would have meant I'd be on the guestlist at a gig in Cambridge, but there we go), and then when that didn't work, I tried just running past the staff and into the venue, which also proved ineffective! I did hang around more-or-less till the end. A few of us huddled by the fire escape and could hear the whole gig – I think we hoped the security could at least let us in for closer 'I Am the Resurrection', but no.

Then the Newport gig came about. I remember it was me, Ade (my brother), and either two or three others – my brother's friend Simon Brown I think, and possibly Max and one of the Thomas twins, or both of the Thomas twins, and not Max – really can't quite remember! But I went to this gig with my Stone Roses 'What the World Is Waiting For' t-shirt underneath a gold Cardiff away top. You honestly did not see many people wearing football shirts at gigs in those days. There were a couple of other people I knew at the gig. I had been to a few gigs at this venue in Newport, but this was probably the biggest of them.

The sound was never fantastic at the Newport Centre, and this proved to be the case again for The Stone Roses. Bear in mind that The Roses were never exactly renowned for the quality of the sound at their gigs. Yes, they were good at creating a buzz and making gigs special, but this was not always because of the quality of the noise they made. If anything, this *Second Coming* tour was viewed as a bit of a conventional move by the band, who usually did things a bit differently – there was supposed to have been a secret tour shortly after the album came out, but this didn't happen after the tour dates became no longer, well, secret.

I had slightly mixed feelings overall about this gig, but it was after they played what I considered to be a really good version of 'Breaking Into Heaven' that I did something which seemed a little bit silly at the time, but which I definitely do not regret now. I decided to take my Cardiff shirt off and throw it onstage! This meant that my Stone Roses shirt was now on display, so I suppose in my head at least, it was kind of me saying after all that the band was more important to me than the football team.

There is video footage on YouTube of this night, and I'm not sure if this footage exactly relates to my memory of what happened next. From what I remember, Ian Brown then lit up a cigarette, and I imagined he was looking straight at me. I then hastily pulled out a cigarette and lit mine (this was when you could smoke at gigs, obviously). It's possible that this happened at a subsequent Ian Brown solo gig, but my memory is that it was at this Stone Roses gig. Shortly after that, what definitely did happen was that Ian Brown picked up the shirt I'd thrown, and put it on! This was definitely one of the biggest 'Oh My God' moments in my life! There were shouts of 'Bluebirds! Bluebirds!' all round the place as, despite being in Newport, obviously quite a few people had made the short journey from Cardiff or the Valleys. He kept it on for a couple of songs I think. The rest of the actual concert is a bit of a blur to be honest.

For what happened subsequently, please refer to the book,

Soul Crew by Tony Rivers! This fine gentleman relates the tale of the riot that occurred, almost certainly as a direct result of the shirt incident. When this was going on, my brother and I were now a few hundred yards away from the venue. I had looked round and saw that it was kicking off. It occurred to me that this must have something to do with what had gone on during the gig, but my brother was having none of it, and was keen for us to just get back to the car and get going. I have a distinct memory of a kind of déjà vu experience I had once we got into the car. I had been in and out of psychiatric units at that time, mainly due to drug taking, and at that time, following an incident where I had imagined I'd had a whole series of visions of the future, I would quite frequently experience the feeling that I was reliving one of these moments. This was one of those times, although it was always a bit confusing – I never really knew what the hell it meant, or whether my brain was just making me think this. Just say no, kids!

Well anyway, the whole incident was picked up by all kinds of music and football magazines. A guy who took a photo of Ian in the shirt made quite a bit of money selling this photo on, I believe. Imagine if it had happened now – everyone in the crowd would have their own photo! Most of the magazines led with the idea that Ian Brown must have been mad to wear a Cardiff shirt in Newport. First of all, despite being a football fan himself, I don't think Ian was necessarily aware that it was a Cardiff shirt. Ridiculous as this might sound, I think he might have simply liked the look of it, as it was golden after all. But secondly, this was a concert, not a football match – there were not likely to be too many hooligans from either side there (though as it happens, obviously, there were a few!) – and again, really, not very often would something like this result in a punch-up. Bear in mind, after all, that I myself had walked into the venue wearing the shirt, and I'd barely given a second thought to it upsetting the locals.

I also went to another gig on this tour, back in Reading. This was more of a sedate event, but at least Steve got to see this gig. One thing I'd hoped to be able to do was to replace the Stone Roses cherub pin badge which I'd bought at the Newport gig, but had then placed on the shirt which I was later to sacrifice that night. Sadly, at the Reading gig, I was told they didn't have any of these badges left, so I never got to replace it. Ade had one, and he wore his in Manchester when he was at Salford University, and would quite often get people offering to buy it off him. I think it's become quite a sought-after badge – there are replicas doing the rounds on eBay now.

It's a funny thing, being the person who threw that shirt onstage. It's just a bit of an odd thing to have as a claim to some kind of fame. A few years later, after The Stone Roses had split up, I designed a t-shirt which had a picture like that of the 'Fool's Gold' sleeve, but with bluebirds instead of the dolphins depicted on the record's artwork. I put 'Cardiff City' where 'The Stone Roses' writing would be, and 'Blue's Gold' in place of the record title. I think this was to tie in, in my mind, with a dance track I'd done at the time which had lyrics based on the Stone Roses song, 'Standing Here'. On the back of this shirt I had a photo of Ian in my Cardiff top, alongside the words, 'Ian Brown is a Bluebird'.

I don't know if too many Cardiff fans really took much notice of the whole shirt thing at the time. Certainly, four years later in 1999, which was when I designed that t-shirt, there were not many people too bothered I don't think. I wore the t-shirt at an away game at Wycombe – on a beautiful sunny day, if I recall – and I don't think many people paid any attention to it, although I do remember Annis noticing the shirt as I walked past him and reading aloud the words 'Blue's Gold' in a curious tone of voice.

This t-shirt was then ruined the first time my mum washed it! I'd had it printed somewhere – not sure what the printing process was – but it basically just fell apart! I had just one more printed which my brother's friend Simon had – I'm not sure if he still has his. I then lost the design I'd done for the front, which was a shame, because it was quite well done, I thought.

So anyway, then it was not until around 2011, when The Stone Roses got back together, having split up in 1996, that there was some revived interest in the shirt throwing incident and what happened. The incident was spoken of in a question (as it happens, from a Newport fan) in the press conference when the band first reformed. You see some Cardiff banners now that relate to The Stone Roses, mainly referencing the lyric from 'I Wanna Be Adored', i.e. 'I don't have to sell my soul' (for obvious reasons) and I don't think you'd see that if it hadn't been for the shirt thing. I do quite like the fact that events at that gig back in 1995 somehow seemed to seal a link between the best band and the greatest team in football! There are fans of other teams who also have banners relating to The Roses, including using the lemon design, but aside from Man Utd, who three-quarters of the band actually support of course, I don't think there's another football team who you could say have a direct link like Cardiff do, as in Ian Brown once wearing their shirt onstage.

By chance, also around the time that the band first got back together, I saw a comment on a webpage relating the tale once more in which someone said they knew who now had the shirt itself. This was a revelation to me, as in all that time, I had assumed it would have been taken backstage – I never imagined someone from the crowd had taken the shirt as the guy in this comment said. I managed to track down the person he referred to and finally had confirmation that he had the shirt. He had picked it up from beside the drum-kit at the end of the night. I still have not yet seen it again despite trying to arrange to meet the new owner. Although I don't imagine I'll ever have it returned to me – not that I necessarily ever thought I would – the new owner did let me know he plans to get the shirt framed, so I like to think that it's at least in safe hands.

Harry & Wembley

In 2005, along with Neil, as mentioned earlier, I made the trip to Austria to follow the Welsh national side. Neil had been to see Wales abroad a few times, but for me, this was my first ever Wales away game. Not too sure why I chose this one particularly – I think the chances of Wales qualifying were pretty much over – but I'd always been told it was a good laugh going to Wales away games, and this definitely turned out to be the case. It really is an experience I would recommend – the social side is fantastic – though I just wonder how much better it would be again to follow a team abroad that actually had a good chance of doing well. At the time of writing, Wales have not qualified for a tournament in my lifetime, although hope springs eternal, especially as we have the most expensive player in the world in our team.

John Toshack had quite recently taken over as manager of Wales again, and I did have some expectations that Wales would do well under him. This didn't really turn out to be the case, but anyway, I did get to meet Toshack, and we had some photos taken with him at the Wales under 21s game while in Austria.

More significantly for me would be the meeting of a fellow fan, when we arrived at the airport in Austria. Harry, a taxi driver from Ely, seemed to be a likeable enough person, and as he wasn't due to meet other friends for another couple of days, we arranged to have a drink with him that evening. I don't know what it was, but I did seem to hit it off with Harry. I think it was mostly his sense of humour. He was a fair bit older than me, but his attitude of not really giving a fuck did make me laugh. Neil and I did most things together while we were over there, and we had a great time, but we encountered Harry a few times, including on the plane back, and then at the airport again when we arrived home. I think the three of us played cards for about an hour before catching the coach back to Cardiff. Neil then slept most of the way, while me and Harry talked for the whole trip back. He just made me laugh.

Over the next couple of years Harry and I became closer friends. Being from Cardiff, Harry was naturally also a City fan. I would still go to The Westgate, and meet up with the regular crowd, but sometimes I would meet Harry as well. During the last couple of seasons of Cardiff playing at Ninian Park, there were a few new faces that Neil and I would meet up with in The Westgate such as Matthew and his dad, Terry, as well as a jovial fellow by the name of Colin. A couple of them had nicknames, such as Swampy. We all got to know each other fairly well, and it was always good to see familiar faces in the pub to talk with about the football. But although I would count them all as friends, I didn't meet up with this group socially outside of the football. It wasn't like the old crew of Neil, Nigel, Steve, me and Blakey.

Nigel now had a large family to support and would be seen only very rarely, Steve was now mostly living abroad while Blakey had been staying in the shadows a bit, also not seen much. There was Rhys, a friend of mine who was also on the scene, but Rhys didn't like drinking, so things could be awkward with him in pubs at times.

Anyway, as things weren't quite the same as they had been, I tended to arrange to meet up with Harry and his friends more. We even went to a few away games together – either Harry or I would drive, and a friend of his, or his grandson or other relatives might come along. They were always quite good fun trips, but even these didn't feel like the old days.

Saying that, one of these away trips has to rank as one of my all time favourite away trips, and that was our trip to Millwall (see next chapter).

Harry and I have travelled together a fair bit over the years. One year we splashed out on a trip to the Algarve to watch Cardiff play in the Algarve Cup. Middlesbrough and Celtic were also involved. Cardiff somehow actually managed to win this mini-tournament, which turned out to be a one-off event, so it is documented that we are the only team to have ever lifted the cup!

We travelled to Spain a couple of times on non-football related expeditions, sometimes doing 'fag runs', but when that became no longer profitable, with the price of cigarettes going up in Spain, we still sometimes made trips to Spain – Harry had a knack of booking ridiculously cheap flights, coupled with ridiculously cheap hotels. Two years running, we went, along with his brother and his brother's wife to a small resort in the north of Spain, out of season, and stayed at a great little hotel which was only about £20 a night all inclusive. Each time, we mostly just spent the three or four days we had there boozing and playing cards.

Neil meanwhile was starting to settle down with Rachael, who he met at a party of mine in fact, and who is now his wife. He was doing fewer away games so I tended to see Neil less. I think it might have upset him that I was not even meeting up with him so regularly at home games – it was a funny situation for me. For so many fans, following football is a matter of strict routine. Meeting Neil and the rest of the Westgate crowd was definitely once a routine for me. Neil and the others would have expected to see me there and, as I was not making an appearance so regularly, it upset Neil's routine. I think it might have upset him on a personal basis, although

I absolutely never intended for our friendship to be affected. With Harry coming from Ely, it was never likely he was going to make it as far as The Westgate to meet for a drink there, so if I did meet him, it would be somewhere in Canton. In more recent years I've just tended to drive and park close to the ground and not even bother having a drink first. My reason for deserting Neil, as it may have been seen, was therefore probably more out of laziness than anything else.

I went on the most recent Wembley trips with Harry, i.e. the Carling Cup final against Liverpool, and the England v Wales qualifying game. Standing next to Harry's grandson Robbie for the Liverpool game, it was great to be amongst one of the best celebrations I've ever been a part of when Turner scored the equaliser. It really was a superb game of football, which Cardiff were unlucky not to win.

For Cardiff's first two appearances at the new Wembley, that is, our FA Cup semi-final appearance against Barnsley, and the FA Cup final against Portsmouth, I'd travelled with Steve. We got extraordinarily drunk on both these occasions. In the first game, we were 1-0 up at half-time, and the feeling of elation at this stage was just phenomenal. The dream, in terms of reaching an FA Cup final, which ten years before would have been unthinkable, was becoming a reality – I remember trying to share this emotion with a Wembley steward, and they seemed to have some understanding of just what this meant for us.

The build up to the final was fantastic, with Cardiff City displays in shops all over the place. We got an early train up, and the boozing began, with me dressed in a cloth cap, with a pipe, an old replica shirt, and a large comedy moustache to look like someone from 1927. Of course, beating Premier League Portsmouth was always going to be a tall order (although they were hardly the giants of the top division, of course), but it was still a shame as we were a little unlucky. Still, it was a fantastic day. There was little of the trouble that had been anticipated – they were calling this the 'people's final' because of the fact that it was two lesser-known teams. In terms of the Cup demonstrating how the dreams of fans of all teams can be realised, here was proof. Harry Redknapp, Portsmouth's then manager, had asked fans of the losing side to stay behind and applaud the winning team – this turned out to be us, of course, and we respected his wishes in doing so.

But Steve and I just got disgustingly drunk. We managed to finally make it back to Victoria Coach Station somehow, and onto the coach (we figured out that going up on the train and back on the coach was the most economical option), only to find that the toilet on this coach was out of order! With no

break for the services, that was one painful journey back, I can tell you, and I think you can imagine the relief on returning to a waiting wall at Cardiff Bus Station.

Although I've only been on the side of the winning team in one of the four times I've been to Wembley, I've enjoyed every trip – they really look after you at the place, it has to be said, and it is one hell of a stadium to watch a game at. Yes, the prices are a bit steep, but for that rare occasion, I'd say it's an experience every sports fan has to try at least once in their lives.

Other trips I've been on with Harry included Wales away against Northern Ireland. We won that 2-1, so it was good to experience what it's like to see Wales win away. I wasn't on my best form on this trip, partly due to some hassle at the place I worked at the time. There were still parts I enjoyed though, including the open top bus trip of the city – it still amuses me when I think back; whereas in most cities it might be, 'Here is the cathedral, dating back to…' on the Northern Ireland trip, a large part of it is, 'And this is where so and so got shot... And that's where so and so got shot...' delivered in a very broad Irish accent! What I also remember that made me laugh was, just before we left for the trip, the sight of Harry getting on the bus and having a right shouting match with a small group of passengers who had taken our places at the front while we had got off to do something else. It just made me laugh that he was giving these poor old pensioners so much abuse when they'd really done nothing wrong.

Harry's one of those people who, like Neil, holds a lot of truck with loyalty. He's an incredibly funny guy, but he has his serious side too. It was always a strain for me that in some senses I'd let Neil down, but just like with everything, sometimes situations change. You can't always cling on to the past. I've tried to find a compromise and see as many of my friends on match day as I can – I might watch the game with Harry, then join Neil for a half-time fag and catch up. Who am I kidding that I'm the important one? Without doubt, the essential point is that I've made some extremely good close friends through the football club. I've made a right tit of myself on a few occasions, but the friends I've made have been incredibly forgiving plenty of times. When I was in hospital around ten years ago, both Harry and Neil visited me more regularly than any other friends, and it's times like those that you realise just who are the most important people in your life.

The Sad Crew Finally Make it to Millwall:

Millwall 3-3 Cardiff: A Classic Remembered

I suppose a trip to Millwall is something every Cardiff fan is expected to do, like a Muslim going to Mecca, at least once in their time as a supporter. It may not apply so much now, but there was a time when both sets of fans were well known for what I heard referred to once as having a 'spiky' following. Even Millwall these days are trying to go more family-friendly, but whatever efforts are made by club officials, there are always still going to be a good number resistant to such changes. Saying that, one thing I do remember is that in fact, Millwall themselves didn't used to travel to Cardiff in large numbers. There was a game ten or fifteen years ago when a large number came down on the train for the first game of the season, but other than that, especially for midweek games in the middle of the season, there were not always many away fans for Millwall games. I did ask a Millwall fan on holiday about this a few years back, and he said it would have been because half of them are in prison. Whether this was true or not, it's the sort of thing you might expect a Millwall fan to say.

So I finally made my first trip there in 2011. A long time past the heyday of the sorts of shenanigans that might be expected, but still, I was expecting a memorable trip, and I wasn't disappointed.

For London games, my friend Harry and a couple of friends would regularly stop at Hounslow West station, where there is free parking, and get a tube in from there. This particular trip did not start well, as while topping up petrol for the trip, due to being stressed because we were running slightly late (I should really have topped up the night before), I somehow managed to walk into the 'door' of the petrol cap, causing it to break off. Could this be an omen for things to come later in the day, I wondered?

We had stopped at a services on the way up. Here, Harry's nephew distributed a couple of fake twenty pound notes he had, buying burgers and getting real money in the change. Driving into the car park at Hounslow West, I found myself driving up a one way street into the exit of the car park, and was informed by the car park attendant that I could receive not three, not six, but nine points on my licence, and could then lose my licence for all the indiscretions, if he just told the police who were in the car park! Thankfully, instead, he then waved us in.

We then made our way across to South Bermondsey station, which is the closest one to the Millwall ground, arriving at around 12pm. This was way before any other Cardiff fans, but Harry wanted to meet a couple of London friends first, and in fact we were late, as he'd arranged to meet at 11.30. I waited with Harry's nephew and grandson who was also with us next to the shops nearby. I must admit, even with three police vans in the vicinity, this was a little scary. We were even wary of opening our mouths for fear that our accents would be detected! Just about every bloke in the area looked and sounded pretty mean. I don't think I have ever been in a place that has more hard-looking bastards per square mile. Except possibly when being among some Cardiff fans, but at least then they're on your side. It was scary but also good fun. We overheard a couple of conversations, and they sounded so authentically like East End mafia types it was unnerving, but comical at the same time. It comes to something when you're wary just of sitting on a wall near to some shops in case this might be considered 'their' wall! We waited in this area in total for around forty minutes for three separate people Harry was meeting, and it was quite a painstaking wait.

From here, we went back to London Bridge as there were no pubs we could see near Bermondsey. We had a quick couple of tokes on a spliff before a couple of pints there. There was a mixture of fans from all different clubs but it was all quite civil. Harry's nephew tried using one of the fake £20s again, and this time was stopped. They called over some police, so he quickly finished his drink and left. We caught the 2.15 'special' train back to South Bermondsey, but he wasn't on it, having to catch a separate train afterwards on his own.

Walking to the ground, there was a mixture of police and Cardiff and Millwall fans. There were a few anti-police chants from the Millwall fans. But really, this did not feel anything like as intimidating as hanging around by Bermondsey before.

We got to the ground, and now for one of the comedy errors of the day. I somehow managed to get myself into one of the Millwall stands! It must have been the end next to the Cardiff section, and I thought Harry and the others were right behind me. I handed my ticket in at the turnstile; I'm through no problem. Suddenly I realise Harry etc. are not behind me. I go back to the turnstiles – no sign. I look around – 'that's not a Cardiff badge!' I thought, looking at one bloke. Very tentatively and quietly, I made my way over to a steward by a fire exit. She looked at my ticket and asked 'Are you a Cardiff fan then?' so I kind of mumbled a reply. She led me out, saying 'We're not going to make a fuss about this!' before leading me past all the Millwall fans and towards where I was supposed to be going in. I did think afterwards that it might have been a laugh staying in the Millwall end. It didn't really occur to me while I was in there as I was thinking more about wanting to go and join the others. Then again, with six goals in the second half, it might have been a tricky one...

Once inside, the place is buzzing. It really took me back to away games of old. The Millwall fans to our left were completely psychotic. Constant threatening gestures, the likes of which I have not seen at any other ground anywhere. We were quite noisy. Noise levels were quite evenly matched I would say, but we were not all completely mental like the Millwall fans. As advised by everyone, 99% of Cardiff fans were not in 'colours' (i.e. replica shirts), but from what I could see, the majority of Millwall fans were not in colours either, which is very unusual. Even those in replica shirts are no 'normal' supporters, though. On the shirt itself it says 'We fear no foe', and they 100% give this impression.

Most of our chants were our fairly standard ones – at least Millwall had a couple that may have been improvised on the day, including a 'You take it up the arse' chant in response to our starting the popular 'We Love You' Ultras-style chant. Before this, I had tried to start 'Are you Brighton in disguise?' but this was not picked up on.

About twenty minutes in, there was a bit of a disturbance amongst some people in the Millwall end down to our left. It looked to me like a dad leading his son out by his ear, and he was then started on by some other men, so around seven or eight people were fighting before all being led out by police. Some Cardiff fans thought it was Cardiff supporters in the Millwall end, and started up a chant in reference to this, but it didn't look like that to me.

The half time score is 0-0. It's not the greatest ever game so far, but it had barely begun in terms of excitement. We check scores from around the ground for bets, etc. before the game gets underway again. The second half is goals and excitement galore. We score first, then Millwall go 2-1 up, then us 3-2 up, before settling for a 3-3 draw. Cracking game it turned out, but in a way, a draw is the worst result for us. A win would have been very handy. If we lost there was talk that Dave Jones might step down, which might mean a better crack at promotion with a new manager. With a draw, we keep the same manager, and promotion is still in the balance. But for this game on its own, it's a good scoreline.

The real talking point of the second half however was when, after we scored one of our goals, a rush at the front of our stand (we were behind one of the goals in the upper tier, which was overhanging an empty tier below) resulted in one fan falling off into the empty seating below. As you can imagine, he must have sustained some very serious injuries. I could not see anything from where I was, but later on during the match, the announcer had the decency to let us know that his injuries weren't life threatening. And in fact, it could easily have happened a second time. After we scored our second or third goal, there was another rush to the front of the tier on my side, which I was among. Someone could quite easily have fallen again, and there was a lot of talk about the wall at the front of the tier not being high enough (although apparently nothing like this had happened before). Millwall fans, as you might expect, had little sympathy. They came up with the idea of a banner depicting a 'no fly zone' for future games.

After the match, we headed out into the car park area, and were kept behind a gate for around forty minutes (relatively standard for away games of old). There were occasional announcements informing us that our train was due to leave at 5.20 (this was a piss-take as we were not in fact let out until around 5.25), and again, that the fan who fell was ok. There was a slight disturbance involving a female fan and some police.

Once we were finally let out, presumably once the Millwall fans had been cleared (God knows what they were getting up to in this time), we were led along a fenced off section, guarded by several police. At one point we passed a place where, a fair distance below us, some Cardiff fans by coaches thought we were Millwall fans, so that was amusing for a while as they hurled abuse at us, until they realised we were both lots of Cardiff fans. It is quite standard to have a police escort to the station, but I don't think I've ever been guarded quite so closely before. It seriously was either fencing or police all the way to our waiting station, and we were not permitted a sniff of a Millwall fan for all this distance.

At London Bridge, the Cardiff fans got off, still escorted. There were a few chants down the escalators; a few tourists filmed us. We stop off at Earl's Court and see a bit of England getting beaten by Ireland in the rugby. Finally back at Hounslow West we find the curry house where Harry and another friend and I had stopped at on another occasion, where I had the legendary 'green' curry. This time we pass on the opportunity.

And there were other things... definitely one of the best away trips I've ever been on, and would recommend to anyone. *Disclaimer: While everything in this section is sadly true, and all the people are real, (though two of the names have been changed), certain people referred to would prefer it to be known that they have never had any affiliation with any group that has gone by the name of the Sad Crew.*

Section 4:

Season 2014/15 – January-May

'Let us never negotiate out of fear.

But let us never fear to negotiate.'

JOHN F KENNEDY

January/February 2015

We were back in blue!!!! It was difficult to come to terms with initially. There was a feeling that order had been restored. Walking around Cardiff, it felt like things were back to how they should be – it really did feel like an enormous weight had been lifted from the collective minds of a lot of people, not just Cardiff City fans, but everyone in Cardiff who had any feelings about the situation, and how the whole thing had just not seemed right. For the first home game back in blue at the stadium, for the first time in a long time, the atmosphere was fantastic. But would the feeling last? Was this really all it would take for the good times to return to the club, or would the fans still demand more – better performances, and better results?

January 10
Bluebirds 1-0 Fulham: Cardiff City fans and the proof of the existence of the soul

I was up early on Friday morning to see that the announcement about whether Cardiff would be going back to blue was due at 2pm. But it didn't come at 2pm. It kind of started coming through around 11am. Every word I'd heard until then seemed to be saying it was going to happen. Then from about midday, it really started coming through. BAM!! There it was on Sky Sports News! BAM!! There it was on the local news! BAM!! There it was coming through on the message boards and the facebook statuses! BAM!! There was the chairman, Mehmet Dalman, confirming it! BAM!! There was Tan's statement with the full details! It was coming through like the healing of an evangelical preacher. It was something like an ecstasy rush; gradual before becoming consuming.

It was pretty much confirmed before 2pm that we were back in blue, and the FA was going to allow it to continue from tomorrow onwards. I'm not even sure anything did happen at 2pm. I never saw a press conference. But then for the next hour or so I felt very strange indeed.

I knew I should be ecstatic, elated, but instead I was still feeling a bit miserable, in fact a bit of a fool. The one person I wanted to be sharing this news with wasn't with me. I'd spent the last couple of nights apart from my girlfriend, thinking we might be splitting up. I was due to see her later in the day, and that's all I wanted now – all I needed was to be with her, and see if we could make it up. I'd sent her a couple of nasty texts and posted something almost unforgivable on facebook. She herself no longer uses it but a number of mutual friends might have seen the post before I quite quickly deleted it in a more sober moment. How could I have been such an idiot? Fortunately for me, one of her best strengths is being incredibly forgiving. I need someone like that because I can do some pretty stupid stuff.

I'd finished the piece I'd been writing on the whole two-and-a-half year campaign to get back to blue (section 2 in this book), and spent a little bit of time contacting newspapers in case any of them would want it. They were all interested but it was too long for them. What did they expect? There was a lot to write about! But now it was just a case of seeing Christina. She had a job interview, and I picked her up on her way over to make sure she could get there in time. It was great to see her, but I knew I was treading on incredibly thin ice. I think I was the first to break the news about the rebrand reversal to her, and she was pretty stunned by it as well I think. Although she's from Bournemouth, Crissy is now a fully-fledged Cardiff resident, and has supported me throughout, even putting up the odd Keep Cardiff Blue sticker herself, and not worrying too much about my irrational hatred of red.

It was all OK now, I told her – the red no longer mattered. I was even happy for red to be the away strip. Any resentment I might have felt towards Tan had dissipated. It was all fine. It was just whether the two of us could sort things out. I dropped her off – we would chat later – and went to get her a ticket for the Fulham game the next day – any excuse to get down to the stadium, to be honest – but I really wanted her to savour the moment with me.

There wasn't quite the rush for tickets I'd expected, but a few people were calling in, one guy getting a ticket for his daughter, and I joked with him about the staff wearing the away colours for some reason. I went to Tesco in Canton to get bread (Brace's – blue packaging), milk (full fat – blue packaging) and a bottle of Cava (not usually an essential item, but today it was!). Everyone I saw seemed happy, people greeting each other with 'Bluebirds!' at any opportunity. I was still on cloud nine, with just my guilt complex overshadowing it.

Crissy was still not out so I popped into The Westgate for a swift pint. It was deserted except for one other guy and we just sat there taking in the situation. Not even sure if he was a Cardiff fan to be honest, but I had a feeling he was. Maybe there were pubs in town packed with people celebrating, but The Westgate was always the pub I'd return to. Where was the party, I wondered? So much for facebook statuses and telling the world via a typewriter how great you're feeling – shouldn't we all be out partying? I guess tonight, you could do what you want, you could go out if you wanted, or stay in and revel in it. Tomorrow was the big day – Saturday the day when football fans come together; friends you haven't seen in maybe a week or two, who you don't necessarily normally socialise with. But when Saturday comes, as they say…

So that night for me was make-up night with the bottle of Cava, talking things through, watching Breaking Bad before going to bed, ready for the next day. We did go out for a short time, and on leaving the flat, maybe not more than an hour after getting in, in the blustery weather conditions, a tree had been blown over right outside my house! Firefighters were at work cutting branches as we ventured out; one car had been hit, and in some ways, I'd wished it had been mine, as it's a bit of an old wreck I wouldn't have minded claiming the insurance on! But this slightly bizarre incident just added further to the surreal nature of the whole day. I was trying to work out exactly what time the tree would have fallen – surely not 19.27?!! The vote to go back to blue the night before had apparently happened at 19.27 – things just got weirder, and the possibility of higher forces being at work had to be a consideration!

Match day came, and the word was out that incredibly, the game might even have to be called off due to concerns of damage to the roof of the stadium. Fortunately it must have been made safe. The only problem for us was we're slow risers and we weren't out the door till 2.20. I had planned to make it to a pub first, but instead we only just made it to the ground in time. We might have made the kick-off but for me fussing around getting a 50/50 ticket – I missed the Bluebirds walking out once again in blue just to save a pound or two on drinks after! And I dropped the ticket in the stadium anyway – unbelievable!

But no worries, we got in, and it was just before kick-off, everyone was on their feet, the Bluebirds were back in blue, and the buzz was back too. It's been debated in Philosophy classes for centuries. Here we go – here was proof that the soul exists. Right here in this stadium. Just a week before it had been a morgue, but now we were the rival of the Sistine Chapel choir, singing the praises of the Boys back in Blue. Just as it should be, the Canton Stand would usually start proceedings, before the whole stadium joined in. Old songs, new songs, borrowed songs, and of course blue songs. After a sticky patch – the first couple of years at the CCS – followed by a trial separation – the rebrand – now, minds, bodies and voices were rejoined in union. All the songs were out for this joyous day. The Bluebirds were risen!

And sing praise for Tan's mum, the person attributed for having coaxed Tan into reconsidering, according to his statement, and realising that reconciliation was the best way forward – the only way forward. Let's hear it for mums everywhere! Blue scarves were raised at every opportunity, and particularly in the twentieth minute of course, the moment now one of celebration rather than a protest, but also, now it was just another part of the whole occasion, rather than the main event.

Just to be able to cheer for the Bluebirds now that they were actually in blue – everything just seemed right, as it should be. It was like the old days, but it was all in context, this is how things are now. We've got this far, and now we continue. Was the singing forced? No, it was all spontaneous. It was like the old days, except in the old days, you wouldn't see nearly as many scarves, and that's one change that can be wholeheartedly welcomed – it looked fantastic!

There was one very sad bit of news and that was of the departure of one of Cardiff's most long-standing stewards, Karen Fiteni, who had passed away on the Thursday night. Ali had announced there would be a pause before the match, and I thought, who on Earth can this be that they're doing this for, this of all games, but when I saw her face, I couldn't believe it. This was the steward who would greet us with a smile at every game in the Bob Bank back at Ninian Park, who would have a joke with Neil every time. Very, very sad, and I wondered if maybe the club had intentionally held off from breaking this news. I even wondered if her departure might have had an influence on the club's big decision the following day, in her memory.

And after all this, there was still a game of football to be played. Not the most wonderful game in the world, but the Bluebirds showed dogged determination following Morrison's early opener, and would not let go of the lead (no pun intended). It was not a bad Fulham side who came to this cauldron – obviously a tough game to play in – but Cardiff's stand-in keeper, Moore, was effective in dealing with the few efforts that were on target. Apparently, the bookies had stopped taking money on Marshall leaving for Everton, but I'd heard since that it wasn't happening, which was a relief of course, though it was nice to know we had a decent replacement keeper. For as long as I've been a Bluebird, the goalkeeper position has been one of our biggest strengths, but if we could keep up solid-enough performances, maybe we wouldn't always have to be quite so reliant on the man between the sticks.

In fairness to Fulham's fans as well, they were no slouches, making a fair contribution. One song alone at the start of the second half went on for at least five minutes. It was just so nice for once to be able to confirm we outsung the away fans at the Cardiff City Stadium. The attendance of 22,000 was maybe not quite as high as some may have expected, with perhaps not enough time for a mad rush of tickets and, let's face it, the £30 walk-up charge was still going to be off-putting to even the more seasoned Bluebird wanting to return to the fray. For me though, this was the best atmosphere I'd been a part of since the opening of the new stadium. Possibly not the loudest – the Scots without a doubt were the cause of that in the Wales v Scotland game in 2012 – but still far, far better than, say, the Man City game, when we were still in red. Sustained noise throughout, as it should be – I didn't even mind the short lull on around the thirty minute mark – you would even get that at Ninian Park during a game lacking in action.

Just to see the looks on everyone's faces. It was a moment to savour. We'd all been part of this, all played a part leading up to this. Maybe it was inevitable that it would come, but still, that made it no less brilliant. Order had been restored. What was wrong was right now. What happened next made little difference because at least everything now felt right. The Bluebirds were back! And a final footnote – there was Frankie on the Radio Wales phone-in afterwards telling us all about how, despite being an invited guest of the chairman, he'd been mistreated by stewards for swearing, sounding exactly like the sort of fan the club may want to be rid of, but to me, and probably anyone else listening, also sounding like a true Bluebird, and you can't just lock people out and expect that to be the solution.

January 24
Cardiff 1-2 Reading: End of the Blue moon, honey?

Following the remarriage of Cardiff City fans and the football club with the return to blue, it now seemed that the brief honeymoon period might be coming to an end already.

One thing the rebrand reversal did not appear to do instantly was inspire fans who had stayed away to return, or just inspire more people in general to come along. Perhaps there were not as many people who were staying away solely because of the rebrand as might have been thought. Maybe the majority who disagreed with it had still been coming along, albeit with a degree of reluctance, because the attendance at our last home game, and the first since the decision was passed, did not dramatically increase. The public had just two days in order to buy tickets, but this shouldn't have been a problem – a game with high demand could of course sell out in two days without any problem.

So the change back to blue was not enough to instantly

bring floods of people to the stadium, and once again with this game, which had an attendance of just 12,000 people, around half that of a typical league game. It would appear that many season ticket holders saw the game as one they could give a miss. It's a funny thing with season ticket holders these days. In years gone by, a season ticket holder was someone who was so dedicated to the club that he or she simply could not miss a single game. These days, I'm sure there are far more season ticket holders who want to go to a lot of matches, but have reasoned that because individual tickets are so expensive, economically, it makes sense to have a season ticket – they therefore have a season ticket for financial reasons, rather than fanatical reasons. This will mean that in some cases, they are going to games out of obligation to their economic reasoning, not their football fixation, hence not feeling the need to turn up to a Cup game which is not included in their ticket.

But that still doesn't make perfect sense as the club had very generously set adult ticket prices for this game at £10-£12, so I really don't see that the ticket price could be a particular influential factor in many people's decision as to whether to attend this game. There could be no boycott as with the previous round's game against Colchester, as that had supposedly been in opposition to the rebrand, which had now been reversed, as per fans' wishes. And indeed, you might imagine that fans may have felt that this gesture on the club's part should have inspired them to make sure they attended this game.

The one marked improvement at the last home game, the first in blue, was the noise levels generated by fans, and the atmosphere in general. Fans at that game certainly showed their appreciation for the club's coming to its senses. A fairly poor display of football resulted in an arguably undeserved 1-0 victory, and it could possibly be said fans assisted in the result.

So it did seem a shame that fans did not return once again to try and inspire another victory for the Bluebirds. Following two successive away defeats in the interim, and more woefully uninspiring displays of footballing ability or lack of it, this certainly could be deemed a contributing factor to the staying away of large numbers of fans. Nonetheless, as it was looking increasingly likely that Cardiff's promotion push would come to nothing, you might have thought people could look to the FA Cup as a last source of hope in the season. But maybe with the standard of football at such a low ebb, many fans truly did not conceive how we could get the win needed to advance to the next stage. But even then, as a fan, should this be a reason to not even attend the match?

The quality of Cardiff's performance in this game could be neatly summarised with one word: dire. So to a large extent, fans' feelings of negativity (despite the feeling of bliss many may have felt only so very recently at the sight of the Bluebirds in blue) could be understood. But unlike at the last home match, the atmosphere at this game could be summed up similarly, i.e. it was not very good. Who am I to conjecture that the two things may not go hand in hand? That if the atmosphere picked up, so might the team's performance, or vice versa? And if the performance picked up just that little bit, would that not increase the chances of winning?

But should it necessarily take the team to improve its skills in order for fans to exercise their vocal chords more? We have seen many low-quality Cardiff City teams over the years, but didn't fans of yesteryear still cheer the team on regardless? One thing I always felt with Cardiff fans was a willingness to just keep cheering for the team, whether or not we were playing well, and whether or not we were winning. A lot of it was simply just to try and put one over the away fans. Quite often in the past, when the opposition scored, to counter the effect of the away fans' celebrations, Cardiff fans would then just keep on singing, quite often even louder than before.

The modern fan seems to have picked up bad habits. These habits include only being willing to sing following a goal and, also, getting very down in the dumps when the opposition scores. Both of these things serve only to play right into the hands of opposition fans, whereas the old habits were to sing throughout and not at any time get demoralised, in a way that might not be considered the standard method of supporting a team, the correct method, but Cardiff fans, I always felt, were not at all standard in their methods of support. The few songs we sing these days are so often much the same as every other club, but this was not always the way. I witnessed something at this game which I felt a little sad about – midway through the first half, one slightly older fan, with his wife or girlfriend, walked down the stairwell, and I think shouted, 'This is not Cardiff', and I believe then was intending to head straight for the exit. Whether he was referring to the team or the fans and the atmosphere wasn't quite clear, but it could have been either or both.

For this game, the club had made the decision of closing the Canton End, which obviously meant that many people who regularly go in this section joined fans in the Ninian Stand (some may also have taken their places in the Grandstand). There may also have been many from the Family Stand who took the decision to switch stands for this game, as although it was open, the Family Stand was pretty empty. It may have been expected that this would improve the atmosphere, with those from the singing/standing stand united with other fans, but this still did not quite work. There were about three rows of fans standing at the back, but even these did not sing all that much. It was just a little disappointing overall.

With the lack of people in the 'sterile area' where usually family of the players and club employees sit between fans in the Ninian Stand (call it the Bob Bank if you prefer) and away fans, this inspired police to make their presence known, and even to capture Cardiff fans on film. A little unnecessary I felt, but you never know, I suppose a few fans may have attempted to traverse the several rows of empty seats in an effort to reach the Reading fans – like trying to cross some heavily guarded river to reach some not-especially-desired destination.

So anyway, during all this, there was a football match, and Cardiff really did not play very well at all, spectacularly dull and uninspiring – Kenwyne Jones' headed goal just about the only noteworthy aspect of the entire game for Cardiff, along with a couple of good saves from Moore perhaps. We just seemed unable to create proper chances that could lead to goals, leading again to a few desperate long range shots from Noone towards the end. The inter-passing, especially in and around the box, was so tediously predictable and lacking in imagination, making it easy for the opposition to deal with. And not just that, but a bizarre number of mistakes in terms of easy passes missed, opportunities spurned due to bad decisions in the final third, and a lack of players giving the player on the ball a wider range of options. Reading were not a good team at all, but still not as bad as Cardiff, and must have counted themselves as lucky to be meeting a City team in as poor form as this. The Cardiff players just didn't look to be enjoying themselves, which is still a contributing factor when playing any sport. If anything, Cardiff, as a team, were getting worse.

I'm sure there were fans in the crowd who were still in good spirits, as I was, with this being just our second home match back in blue. And yet very soon this will seem normal once again. Common sense may have won, but quickly things will be as you were. There was a sense at the last game that it was like watching Cardiff in the old days, not just pre-rebrand, but even like it was back at Ninian Park, when the standard of football was not always the greatest, but the buzz was still always there. The only thing remaining was to see exactly how fans would respond when there was a bigger crowd for the next home league match.

February 17
Cardiff 1-1 Blackburn: City Seal Draw with Smash and Drop

The one-time Premiership champions came to Cardiff off the back of a 4-1 FA Cup win over Premier League mainstays Stoke, so if this was to be the first league win in six for City, it was not going to be easy. On the flip side, it was likely that the Lancashire team might have some hangovers following the win over their Staffordshire rivals, and that this game might be of lesser concern to them, so if City could up their game for once, was this one for the taking?

Blackburn certainly did look a little on the lacklustre side. Like City, their play-off hopes were now pretty dubious, but unlike City, they could be pretty sure of safety from relegation, so a win for them might be of as much use to them as they made it look on the pitch. They didn't really bother to build attacks, relying more on the odd counter attack when City spurned possession, which to City's credit, they were not doing much.

Without doubt, this was too little too late by Cardiff, but there were some promising signs, as they played some quite reasonable possession football, with fewer mistakes than in previous games. There were a couple of quite useful-looking stages of attacking play in the first half; enterprising and inventive, you could almost say. It's a team that looks a bit incohesive – there are players who don't seem to know what the other players' functions are exactly, or don't know quite where or how to put the ball, because they don't quite know who is going to get on the receiving end of it, how, or perhaps even, why. But whether it was more from luck than judgement, the ball was passed around a bit, and the ball was getting forward.

Cardiff appeared now to be playing with some kind of wing formation, with Noone on the left and Kennedy on the right, though neither of them are exactly wingers in the classic sense, each a tiny bit too clumsy. It looked to me as if Noone was under instruction to just keep running once he had the ball, even if this meant eventually running into a tackle and giving up possession (this happened frequently), or running into a tackle and gaining a free kick. If this instruction was to garner more of the latter, I suppose it could work as a form of strategy, but many was the time that I would have preferred Noone to make sure of keeping possession by getting an effective pass in.

Crosses into the box again proved a very problematic area for Cardiff. There didn't look to be one Cardiff player who could be consistently relied upon to deliver good crosses, and when on the rare occasion a good cross was made, there was then not one Cardiff player who was always there, in the right spot, to receive the ball and make something of it. So this tactic may as well have been abandoned, and instead, Cardiff should have concentrated on making runs into the box, and making more effort to pass the ball into the net. Crosses and volleys are just a little beyond this side at the time.

With the new players in, at last we could say that this was a little more like Slade's own side, but it was now too late in the season to think about what the team could start doing or what effect it could have. But it would have been nice if they could have just continued showing more of the kind of work rate that was put in for this game, and more of this kind of enthusiasm.

Once again, the crowd was a little sparse and on the quiet side, but spirits in the crowd were lifted as the team started playing a bit better. So there was a sense that the crowd and the team were responding to each other. I found it a bit sad that, it appeared, maybe 4,000 season ticket holders were just not turning up now that there was little to play for. Officially it's not allowed, of course, but didn't each of these season ticket holders have friends they could lend out their tickets to, to increase the numbers in the stands? It might never happen, but I wondered in fact if there was a way the club could allow this – more people in the stands can only ever be a good thing?

It was only into the second half that things really started coming alive, and a couple of shots got fired in. Gunnarsson's shot in the sixty-fifth minute got the blue torch paper lit. The ball fell to him outside the box, and taking a shot looked the right option; it was hit hard, and not too far over. Blackburn retaliated with a shot against the run of play on around seventy-five minutes. Then finally the goal Cardiff fans had been calling for came on around the eighty-fifth as Morrison headed in from Whittingham's corner, and now a slightly unexpected victory was surely in the bag.

But no, sadly this team clearly could not quite get their heads round the concept of winning a game, and even let this lead slip. Fans had sung the team's praises, but for some reason, just as the ball was in our own half, the 'Come on, City' chant was aired, which didn't seem quite right to me. In the current climate, with fans not often in singing mode, it sometimes seems like any chant that gets going must be worth singing along to, but isn't this the chant usually reserved for when we're chasing the game, not when we've just taken the lead? So suddenly, we're singing 'Come on, City' with minutes to go, there's something not quite right about it, and the next thing, Blackburn score!

Sickening might be one word, disappointing another; downright f'ing stupid might be one further way of putting it. Just keep the ball out! The ball was cleared off the line, but then somehow fell to ex-Cardiff man Gestede, who's gone on to great things at Blackburn of course, and the next thing, we've thrown two of the points out of the bag and are left with just the one. Just stupid – I'm sorry, but that's what it was.

Yes, Doyle looked sharp (and given a good ovation when substituted); yes, Kennedy looked ok; yes, the backline of Malone, Manga, Morrison and Peltier looked very effective; yes, each player seemed to have upped their game, each feeding off the confidence of the other, urging the whole team on... but still, not all that many real goalscoring opportunities, and still, not quite the confidence to make sure of a win that was there for the taking.

Blackburn looked alert, but genuinely not that concerned

about the result, and City just did not quite have the wherewithal to take advantage. It was good to see ex-Cardiff players Gestede (though not good to see him score) and Conway, battling hard as ever. This Rovers team was not going to do us the favour of just rolling over, but sadly, instead of completing the smash and grab, it was more of a smash and drop.

February 28
Cardiff 0-1 Wolves: Tan Shows in Blue, But Whitts sees Red

There was one slight snag with the club's initiative for this match encouraging fans to wear retro replica shirts. It was still fecking winter! People are still wearing three or four layers of clothing! No doubt in the warmth of pubs before and after the match, with coats dispensed of, replica shirts could be exposed, but inside the stadium, not many were seen as fans kept coats on to avoid exposure to the elements.

If the initiative was to get more people to attend the game, this was also a failure, as once again, there were an alarming number of empty seats. Yet again, many season ticket holders must have simply stayed away. Even our recent 'mini-run' was clearly no inspiration, but of course, four draws and one win is not exactly going to instil a massive amount of confidence, and the quality of the football – Gunnarsson's goal in the last game aside – had still not picked up. Add to that the fact that the atmosphere at home games was still a little tepid, plus the fact that there was little left for Cardiff to play for this season, and you had all the ingredients for understandable numbers of stay-aways, whether or not it did indicate a lack of loyalty.

One person who did manage to make his first game of the season was a certain Mr Vincent Tan, proudly wearing his home shirt (this season's). Tan was on hand to shake fans' hands and give photos before the match, and was apparently back in favour, despite the fact that reports this week have said we're something like £150 million in debt, and most of this, as far as I could make out, was to Tan himself.

A good number of other people in attendance were Wolves fans, who loudly made us aware of their presence. Fixtures with this lot have always been feisty affairs – there was the time when our fans were banned from their ground – and although there has rarely been any trouble at Cardiff matches in recent years, there were rumours of some fighting outside the ground before the start of this game.

Although there were a lot of them, I didn't really think all that much of the Wolves support. There have been far better travelling fans at the CCS, even if they have not travelled in such large numbers. This lot's obsession was to keep singing the English rugby song, which was a bit pathetic, and when they then sang the English national anthem, particularly so close to St David's Day, this was just piss-taking of the highest order. On the twelfth minute of the match, fans all around the ground joined in a minute's applause for the poor twelve-year-old lad who was run over near to the ground, and the Wolves fans did join in this, but that aside, they had about as much respect as Frankie Boyle at a comedy awards ceremony.

Cardiff fans were resolute in their determination to not rise to the rugby taunts – if it was Swansea playing Wolves of course, the immediate response would be to sing 'Hymns and Arias' right back at them. But no, that's not what we do at Cardiff, which unfortunately leaves us without a sufficient retaliatory response.

The feistiness continued onto the pitch, in a gritty game which saw Cardiff enjoy much of the possession in the early stages, but still without much of an end product in front of goal. Instead, Wolves scored in pretty much their first attack of any significance. We contained things for the duration of the half, and came out much better after the break, but could never quite make the necessary breakthrough.

The most telling moment of the second half was the sending off of Peter Whittingham – the first time he'd seen red in his entire career. Whittingham is a player who generally has always walked into the first team, and of course has been a loyal servant of the club for many years, and yet in recent times some fans had been turning on him. The main reason to keep him in the side was that he's always been the principle taker of corners and free kicks, but perhaps a little less effectiveness in this area, and his becoming more lax as an outfield player, led to criticism from fans. Yes, some of the set pieces had been a little off, but to be honest, without someone who could be relied on to get on the end of even his good deliveries, what else could he do? It wasn't that long ago that Whittingham was on such good form some fans spoke about how he could follow former Cardiff striker Bothroyd in getting an England cap. He's a player who's always gone in and out of form, but it won't help if players around him don't put in the effort and make use of his assists.

Managers never seem to like doing the sensible thing of substituting players who are already on a yellow card to ensure they don't pick up a second and a dismissal – is it seen as a cowardly tactic? Whatever, Kenny Jackett took off Iorfa, who had one booking, and seemed to be itching for a second, whereas Slade kept Whitts on, thus letting him make his absurdly reckless challenge moments after Iorfa's replacement had taken to the field – ensuring his forced removal.

If City's hopes of getting anything out of this game seemed meagre with ten against promotion-chasing Wolves, ironically, Whitts' dismissal actually meant that the remaining players really pulled their socks up and buckled down. We finally saw some quite good efforts on goal, and at one point, I thought the ball had breached the Wolves' goal-line, but sadly not.

There were some who said that this was one game City deserved to win, but to be quite honest, I wasn't so sure myself. Yes, we had a fair bit of possession, but the play for me was still too static and predictable. Wolves were relatively comfortable, and we did not do enough to really rattle their cage. And yet again, if it was not for Marshall in goal (who had not been heralded so much in recent games, despite keeping the opposition goal tally to just three in the last five games), we could easily have conceded one or two more, whereas our attacks were never good enough for it to be true to say we were unlucky. The problem as I saw it was that there was still no-one on the pitch who you could point to and say – there is someone who we can rely on to consistently get goals. If we were going to score, it seemed more likely that it would come from a fluke or some rare stroke of individual genius.

Things could have been worse – we could have been rooted to the bottom of the table like Blackpool, who were also in the Premier not so long ago. Blackpool had apparently fielded a total of fifty different players over the course of the season, but, it seemed, were yet to find a group of eleven that could hack it in this league. Cardiff had also made many changes to the line-up; could we eventually settle on a team that would finally gel and gift fans the inspired performance craved rather than the insipid seen so often?

March

Some people, it would seem, are never happy. So many people had campaigned for a return to blue, and even now this had been achieved, fans were still staying away. Where were all the people who had promised to return if the rebrand was reversed? Come to that, where were the people who had season tickets regardless? Large numbers were staying away. Promotion was now out of the question but were fans expecting too much of this season? After so many years of success – two Wembley Cup Final appearances, plenty of play-off drama, promotion to the Premier League – surely we could live with one year of mediocrity? For many, it seemed, no, we could not. It had to be more glory, or nothing. Perhaps the football had got a bit boring – but so had the fans, it seemed to me – at home at least, we'd become a lifeless set of fans, sucking the enjoyment out of the experience for so many, and forcing them to stay away.

March 7
Is This the Modern Season Ticket Holder?

On the afternoon of Cardiff's home game against Charlton, I met someone at the bar in Chapter Arts Centre who I thought could possibly be typical of the new breed of season ticket holder at Cardiff City. There must have been between 5,000–8,000 season ticket holders who, in this later stage of the campaign, were not regularly going to matches, and perhaps hadn't been for the last three or four games. The person I spoke to in Chapter did go to the day's game against Charlton, but that was the first game he'd been to in four. And all he did was moan.

I happened to be in Chapter for something, and was surprised to see so many Cardiff fans having a drink there before and after the match. I really didn't expect it to be the sort of place football fans would go to for a drink. I realise it's in Canton, and not that far from the ground, but the ambience of the place is not necessarily suited to what you might call the typical football fan. You'd expect it to be a place for people who have a little bit more money, and I suppose, it's people who have a little bit more money who you might imagine have latched onto the club more recently, since its rise to the Premier League.

The first thing I said to this person when talking about the match, which I hadn't been able to go to due to my commitment at Chapter, was that we could perhaps finally write off hopes for the play-offs, following the disappointing 2-1 defeat. This was meant to be in reference to the fact that Sean Morrison had said it wasn't out of the question that Cardiff could go on a run at the end of the season, like Reading did a few seasons back when Morrison was with them. Really, it was just meant as a bit of a joke, as people I think had been jokingly talking of Cardiff's prospects in the last few weeks following our recent 'mini-run' (one defeat in seven, wow!).

I'm not sure if this person could detect that I was joking, or knew what I was referring to. Maybe he was just pissed off after the result, but instead of laughing along, he took it upon himself to try and wind me up, as if I knew nothing about the club or the game. He asked about a couple of games from as far back as January, and I couldn't remember if I'd gone to them (they meld into one a bit for me). I think he assumed that I was not someone who went regularly to matches, and thought this was a good opportunity for mickey-taking.

I told him that I actually had a season ticket (albeit one quite recently acquired), and he didn't seem to care too much about this. I told him that I didn't think Slade was the main problem, but that Solskjaer should have been sacked at the start of the season, not ten games in or whatever it was. He seemed to think Solskjaer wasn't even the manager at the start of the season. He could remember as far back as January, but apparently not back to the start of the season!

In some ways, I wish I had been someone who knew nothing about the club. I would have really liked to see how someone who is claiming to be an ambassador for the club goes about trying to belittle a stranger who has a passing interest in the day's result.

I wasn't able to establish just how long this person had been a season ticket holder; whether he was a new fan or a long-time fan, but either way, I just found it bizarre that things had got to this stage; where season ticket holders might be no longer proud to talk about their own club, where they have absolutely no optimism about any hopes for the season, where they attend just one in four games, and don't seem to enjoy the games they do go to.

What is the point in having a season ticket if you're not even making use of it? Surely the point of a season ticket is so that if you're going to go to, say, at least three games in four, you'll save money. If you're going to skip the games when the weather's bad, you're not in the mood, or the rugby's on, how can you then try to mock someone who enquires about the day's result? Is that really what season ticket holders are like these days? Are they just people who have got enough money to chuck around so that they can brag to work colleagues they own a season ticket, which is oh so great when we're doing well, but when we're doing badly, what then? Well, of course, you can still brag you've got a season ticket, but if you don't go to the games, who is really going to know or care?

In the old days, and I'm talking when there were 4,000 people at Ninian Park, if you met someone who had a season ticket then, it was a rare thing indeed, and such people were much respected and revered. They were known as total lunatics. If you had a season ticket then, let's face it, it meant that you were such a passionate fanatic that really, you had little choice but to have one.

It seems that the modern season ticket holder is just someone who sees it as an investment, like buying a computer, or a second-hand car. It's a convenient method of payment. It's not a thing to treasure. It can be something to brag about, but it's not a badge of honour any more.

What saddens me as well is that everyone is fully aware that, while you're not supposed to, season tickets are easily transferrable – the machines on the turnstile (another aspect of the soul-sapping nature of the new stadium) – are not going to recognise if it's Joe Bloggs using Joe Bloggs' season ticket or not. So when the modern season ticket holder is unable to go to a match for one reason or another, why can't he at least lend his ticket out? Does the modern season ticket holder have no friends? Not even a work colleague who he is forever bragging to about his season ticket holder status? Instead, it seems that a lot of these season tickets are just staying in their owners' fat wallets, only to be removed when the sun is shining and the modern season ticket holder has no shopping to do. There's no getting away from it, having a season ticket is a pretty big commitment – getting to all, or most games, is no mean feat, but make some kind of effort, eh?

There's always the option of the club following Swansea's lead (pains me to say it) and introducing a form of part season ticket. I think they have an option there where you can buy something like a block ticket that means to some extent you can pick and choose your games, rather than having to go to every game. Maybe that would suit some better?

The reason I couldn't attend the game against Charlton was that I'd signed up to take part in a Zombie School, which meant I'd be entitled to a free ticket when the Zombie Apocalypse came to town a couple of weeks later. I couldn't help think of the irony to be honest. While I was roaring around a nearby park learning how to act like a zombie, not too far away was a stadium full of them, i.e. season ticket holders (the ones that could be bothered to turn up) sitting there like zombies, except for the odd banshee-like groan or moan, and then the players, not much better, chasing the old pig's bladder, looking so gormless and clueless that they wouldn't have had to do too much acting at the Zombie School.

In fairness to the 'teacher' (Boss Zombie) at this school, he was excellent, and got fifty or so non-thespians running around in a pretty authentic zombie-like manner in no time, and actually enjoying themselves. Everyone in the group was treated respectfully, no-one was held up to account. An extremely well-managed programme, and Cardiff City's coaches could learn a few things from this guy.

Of course, times were tough at Cardiff; no-one was over the moon about things, but let's face it, it had been a long time since we'd had to endure any hard times. Just look at what we've had in the last few years – four Wembley appearances, two Cup finals, promotion to the Premier – surely we could endure one tough season, when after all, at least it looked likely that we were safe from relegation?

I'd been saying it all along (readers may be tiring of hearing it!), but I was still of the opinion that fans needed to be looking at themselves rather than forever blaming others. There were many who were now saying they would be turning their backs on the club and walking away next season, and in some ways, who could blame them, the way things were? But the truth was, there were a couple of thousand who had tickets for the 2014/15 season who had already started turning their backs.

The most positive thing I could think of was, you never know, perhaps once the more spineless fans had been weeded out, the good times, where people actually enjoyed going down and it was a good, fun, sociable occasion instead of just a load of moaning goons, perhaps once we've had a bit of a cull, then maybe the good times might return.

March 14
Brentford 1-2 Cardiff: A Tale of Not Missing the Bus

Well this felt more like lower league football. Older Bluebirds might recall many games against Brentford, who always seemed to be vying for promotion at the same time as us. The main game that would be remembered was of course the game when maybe four thousand City fans made the trip along the M4 one bank holiday when inexplicably, the game was made pay-on-the-gate, a rarity for Cardiff games in those days.

I was amongst the large number who travelled up and was not able to get in. I drove all the way down, milled around the streets for a while before it became pretty apparent that, with the away end filled, despite pleas to let us into a section of the home stand, these pleas would fall on deaf ears. There were concerns that things might turn nasty, but instead, most fans simply shrugged their shoulders and flocked into pubs or just went home, as I did.

Fifteen years later, I was to finally see the inside of Griffin Park, though I almost didn't make it this time after missing the coach I was booked onto with Carl Curtis. I was allowed onto one of the Supporters coaches instead.

Griffin Park, I learned, is unique in being the only ground in England with a pub on each corner of the ground – makes sense you would think. The person who told me this was unsure whether any Scottish grounds share the same benefit – let's face it, it would be less of a surprise in Scotland.

I sampled just two of the pubs (with Fosters £4 a pint in one). I met a couple of London mods in the second, wearing trademark Jam t-shirts and target badges, who turned out to be Cardiff fans. One of them had Welsh family, hence his support for the Bluebirds, although whether they were seasoned fans, I wasn't too sure – they were unaware of the existence of the (now defunct) London-based 1927 Supporters Club. Not even sure about their credentials as fans of The Jam, apparently also unaware that 'the other two' now went under the name of, erm, Of The Jam. Nice enough lads, nonetheless, but I couldn't stay and chat for too long as I had to leave to head for the ground early-ish to meet up with the ever-reliable Vince Alm for my ticket.

Vince had recently posted up a quite graphic view of football from the past – there was no fighting that I saw at this fixture, but here was a ground for those hankering after the old days, with proper terracing just like Peterborough's London Road. I guess for some lower league teams like Wycombe or Barnet, Griffin Park might seem quite sizeable, but now Brentford have finally made it to the Championship, I was told that within a couple of years, Brentford will be joining the legions of teams that form a part of 'modern football', with a shiny new stadium, with lots of shiny new seats and presumably even more ludicrously priced tea and coffee than that served in their present stadium. Brentford's progress in recent years may have stalled somewhat and been a little slower than ours, but it seems they may finally be on their way up, whether to better things or not is open to debate.

With almost an hour to spare before kick-off, I had plenty of time to relish being amongst like-minded others on an old fashioned terrace. There were many other fans who'd taken their places early, and we had a good old sing-song pre-match. Chris Kamara walked past at one point and did a one-handed ayatollah. Personally, I would say, if you're going to do a one-hander, you might as well not bother at all, but he did have the excuse of having a clipboard in his other hand.

The Bluebirds ran out and we were treated to a couple of good shots from the goalkeeping coach, Martyn Margetson – who I didn't realise had returned to Cardiff – and we wondered if the club had ever considered given him a try out as a striker.

By the time the match started, both fans and team alike were well up for this one. When there's nothing much left to play for, you might as well just go for it, and enjoy yourselves if you can. Fair play to Cardiff, they showed an eagerness of spirit so often lacking when there was still hope for the season. Maybe it was the lack of nerves, but there was far less hesitancy. It was hard to pinpoint exactly what the Bluebirds were doing right that was better, but I think it basically just stemmed from increased confidence, leading to more flowing football. Brentford, hanging on to a play-off place, looked by far the more cautious.

That said, things did not look good when Moore (formerly a keeper for Brentford) sadly gifted the home team the opener. After Pritchard had shot directly at him, he palmed the ball into the waiting path of their striker, Gray, who tapped the ball into the back of the net. This prompted Bees' fans to finally wake from their apparent slumber. Some fans to our right actually stood up, and spread arms out wide (some even were apparently praising Moore by bowing down to him). Slightly comical that it had taken half an hour, and a goal, for them to alert us to their presence. Most sat down quite quickly, but one joker remained standing, and henceforth was the plaything of the City fans, dancing around, and doing the ayatollah for us when prompted. He even showed us his lovely bare chest – I think if we'd asked him to strip naked and run round the pitch, he'd have done it. Not sure how happy other Brentford fans were to have an apparent Cardiff convert in their midsts.

Half-time was a ruck of bodies out back, a health and safety inspector's worst nightmare, but really, as long as common sense was used, of course no-one was going to get hurt. I like the fact that Brentford allow for a large smoking area. What they don't allow is for people to leave the ground, as you might like to do to visit a more accessible pub toilet, or perhaps get a beer, with alcohol not being served within the ground. Everyone was told that if they left, there would be no re-entry, yet a couple of dozen City fans, who appeared to have had enough, did leave nonetheless.

To be quite honest, I felt this was a little insulting to us remaining fans – did they honestly have so little faith in the result being turned around? I overheard a couple of lads say they hoped we could go on to win to prove the fans that had left wrong, and as fate would have it, that's exactly what City went on to do.

Perseverance was the key to winning this match. No fancy football, just sticking to the task of going for first equaliser and then winner, without giving Brentford much of a sniff in the meantime. Fans' favourite Fabio was ever-present, making things happen. Up front, Macheda, who had hit a little bit of form at last, with a goal in each of the last three games. Here, his task was to knock in a simple enough effort after a mistake from Brentford's keeper. Seemed a shame that only now, late in the season, he'd found his scoring touch. Meanwhile Le Fondre on loan at Bolton was also scoring goals – could things finally work when Le Fondre returned and the partnership was reunited, or perhaps it was the fact that the two didn't play well together that was the problem all along?

Fans went into an advanced stage of revelry when a little over ten minutes later, Revell chipped the keeper from outside of the box to score the goal that would seal it for City, though few would have been certain of this at the time, or indeed with ten minutes to go, when Cardiff were reduced to ten following Harris's very harsh dismissal. When Macheda was given his marching orders two minutes from time, the victory seemed even less certain, particularly when it was then declared there would be six minutes added on.

After four hours of being on my feet, I wouldn't have minded being substituted myself, as I'd started to get a big of cramp, but then again, I would not have liked to be in the fans' changing room and missed the end of this one. With what few remaining fingernails that Cardiff collectively held between them, somehow they clung on – fortunately former Cardiff man, Tommy Smith could not score for Brentford at the death – and henceforth the celebrations proper could begin. Of course, it was 'Nine men, we only need nine men' all the way to waiting buses and cars.

Nine men we needed for this one, and now, without nine wins out of nine, there was surely no way Cardiff could still make the play-offs, and even then it wouldn't be anything like certain, but all we could do was take one game at a time, and see what might happen.

This was a great one for all Cardiff fans, both 'dressers' and 'normals' alike. I had to make my apologies to Carl Curtis again; for blogging purposes, I thought I should at least try out his coach, which I expect is more for the 'better attired' style of fan. But if access to this coach involves nothing more than buying a ticket – don't know about you, but I always felt to be 'welcomed into the fold' you needed to do a little bit more perhaps by way of proving worthiness first – and yet, despite buying a ticket, I still couldn't get myself on board, maybe this was fate decreeing that I would never mix it among this type of fan, and would always be just a 'normal'!

Then again, show me a normal Cardiff City fan – you've got to be a bit crazy to go through everything we go through haven't you?!

March 17
Cardiff 1-1 Bournemouth: Hold the three Cherries!

There had been a fair bit of discussion on message boards before this game about Cardiff's away support this season. We stood fifth from bottom in the league of average away attendances, which on the face of it does look pretty bad for a team that's just come down from the Premier. We took a good travelling support to Brentford, and mitigating circumstances for the low mean figure included us having had a lot of long distance midweek games, but nonetheless, the figures still didn't look all that great.

Of course, it hadn't been the best of seasons, so you might expect numbers to drop. Perhaps something to bear in mind is that while there might always be a lot of fans who would like to go to more away games, money has to always be a factor. People can't always afford it, it's as simple as that. One thing that fans are doing a lot more of these days is gambling. Gambling's everywhere, with more adverts on TV for betting websites, poker websites, and new betting shops springing up everywhere. If you're a bit low on funds, you might put a couple of bets on, and whether or not you win might dictate whether you can then justify something like an away trip. Then in the cases where you lose, funding that trip becomes more of a dilemma.

We met up before the match at Les Croupiers casino. We had planned to go to the Sand Martin, but it was a bit crowded – a Wetherspoons in town, on steak night, might have been the better option. But instead, it was the Croups, a popular place for a pint, but of course, once you're in there, it's difficult to resist the temptation to put a few quid on something, and before you know it, you've lost another five or ten quid, and it's become a costly pint. One bloke apparently turned something like £100 into £3,000, but these are the exceptional cases of course, and who's to say he didn't go on to lose most of his profit? Always tough to walk away…

With kick-off approaching, at least that made the decision to leave the place easier. If the drop in away crowds was a bad sign, the consistently bad showing by fans at home was no better. Optimism was some way off its peak, but nonetheless, with odds of nearly 4/1, a mate and I had bets on a Cardiff win tonight. We'd shown some improvement in recent games, I felt, a bit more belief, and after all, we had nothing to lose in this game – the pressure was on Bournemouth, who needed to keep getting the results in their final push for promotion, although they were a team playing as if they were under no pressure whatsoever; a side brimming with confidence, but nonetheless, I really did not want to see these minnows in footballing terms do a treble over us. I hoped the team felt the same way, and would want to have a pop at the Cherries and burst their bubble.

Bournemouth's football was all about passing and moving; it was a fast, attacking style which City initially did not seem to have much of an answer for – we might have been statues out there on the pitch for all our effectiveness in retrieving the ball. On sixteen minutes, the man of the moment, Harry Arter was given a tiny bit of space and sent a thunderball of a shot flying into the net which Moore could not get near. It seemed like the writing was on the wall and the Bluebirds were going to be a fresh victim of a thumping defeat at the hands of Eddie Howe's men.

But personally, I wasn't giving up hope. As long as it remained 1-0 to the away team, there was no reason why we couldn't try to muscle our way back in. Cardiff actually had a number of chances in the first half. Our football wasn't as good to watch but we came close a few times. The ball was laid up perfectly for Revell, but he fired way over. Noone had a shot that was not too far away, and then Revell again could have scored, but elected to pass instead of shoot and that opportunity was spurned. We won a good number of corners, and it felt like we deserved something for our efforts.

The referee made this game even more of a spectacle with quite a few pretty odd decisions, though they definitely were not always wrong. There were two or three corners given that surely couldn't have been corners, there were a couple of fouls on either side that were given that looked as if they shouldn't have been, and a couple that weren't that perhaps should have been. We had a drop ball, and then in the second half, we were spared some embarrassment when the ref disallowed a goal for Bournemouth, ruling that Moore had been obstructed when he kicked right at Callum Wilson, who then put the ball in the net after it rebounded off the cross bar.

We were lucky on a couple more occasions, with two goal-line clearances which kept us in the game. But that's not to say Cardiff did not continue where they left off in the first half; we kept on pressing, continuing to test Bournemouth. Noone had a good run, before passing to Gunnarsson, but his shot was straight at Boruc, Bournemouth's man between the sticks.

Fans had been customarily quiet for most of the game – we didn't even sing 'We'll Always be Blue' on 19:27 – was it for the first time this season? (I missed Charlton, so not sure if it was sung at that one). This was in stark contrast to the travelling promotion-chasing Cherries' support, but we were just singing at them 'Where were you when you were shit?' when the breakthrough came, Manga scored from a corner, fans were on their feet, and all of a sudden, there was a game on.

Yes, it can be quiet at home games, but one thing we sometimes do is suddenly get behind the team. I remember seeing this against Leeds a few years back at the CCS and being pretty impressed. We might be silent for 60 minutes, then something in the game turns, and we're on our feet, the noise level suddenly increases, it's like a tidal wave effect, which I think can be very intimidating. When Cardiff stand up, the away fans shut up, and that's exactly what we got Bournemouth to do. All of a sudden, it's as if the ball, the team, the fans, the spirit of the stadium, are united as one, it's like we're ruling, and even if it's just for a couple of minutes, we're in control and totally bossing things. This happened in the five or ten minutes after our goal. Who cares if it takes a goal for this to happen, when it happens, it's like a great surge, a gambling win, a drug rush, sex. That feeling of yes, we can do this, comes back, and it can be pretty good.

Well, we didn't quite do it this time, but fair play, we gave it a good go, and we stopped Bournemouth in their tracks at least. I have to say, I was very disappointed by our strikers in this game. There were some good performances in most areas from the likes of Connolly, Morrison, Kennedy, Fabio, Manga, Gunnarsson and Whitts – just about the whole team bar the front two. Jones was slow, and just did not look effective even when he got into good positions; Revell made too many errors in my view. I think one or other of them should have come off a lot sooner; Doyle should have been given more than just a couple of minutes to try and get a winner.

I was saddened to see yet another fan being taken out of the stand by the heavy-handed security. This followed a female fan being made to leave in the game against Charlton, for doing not much more than standing up. Is this excessive treatment really needed when we should be doing our best to keep loyal fans?

As the game drew to a close, a lot of people seemed content with a draw in this game, but I still think (maybe just because I had a bet on it) that we could have done a bit more to really go for a win. This result made it just two defeats in ten, which was quite a big improvement. If we'd just avoided that terrible slump around Christmas time, we could still have been in contention. Then again, I was still of the view that if we'd started the season with a new manager instead of sticking with Solksjaer, things might have been different. In general, the word at this point was, let's carry on making progress and see how we can shape up for the next campaign.

March 21
Cardiff 2-0 Birmingham:
For Some A Tan, For Others, A Ban

The stellar performance of the day came from the sun. With the moon out of the way (it was the day after the lunar eclipse), the sun was having a good old shine, allowing everyone to have a go at topping up their Vincents. It felt like being at a pre-season friendly, especially with not so much riding on the game for either team, although as it turned out, things would get less friendly towards the end of the match.

A couple of changes to the side for this one; Marshall was back in for Moore; with Connolly out on loan, Malone was back, looking eager, especially in the first half, to try and reclaim a first team place; Fabio was put on the right instead, and Ralls was also given a start, and like Malone, was getting in amongst things to prove his worth, with a couple of good runs into the box early on. Anyone who was expecting the return of Macheda would have been disappointed though; he pulled up in training just prior to the match, and so Jones and Revell were kept up front. Personally, I would have quite liked to have seen how a Macheda/Doyle partnership might have worked out.

I didn't think much of the Birmingham side in the 0-0 draw back in November, and there was little sign that they'd made much progress since then. Just as in the away fixture, Cotterill got some stick due to his spell at Swansea, despite hailing from Ely in Cardiff. Against a poor team, it did not look like the fanciest football was going to be required to get something out of this game.

With the standard not the greatest of shakes, and the crowd suitably non-plussed, it gave me time to reflect on a few things. I kept wondering what was needed to re-instil some enthusiasm in the home crowd. It's all very well keeping on saying that the football isn't entertaining enough. I'm not saying that an exciting front man to pin our hopes on wouldn't help, but had Cardiff fans' expectations become too great?

For so long we were told about this mythical 'promised land' that we were aspiring to. Does anyone know what that was exactly? And it occurred to me that the journey, striving to reach the promised land, was the fun part. If the promised land was a new stadium and reaching the Premier, well we got there, but the new stadium has proved a bit of a flop and as for our Premier League adventure, this was hardly what you might call having time in the sun, as it were, more like a disastrous package holiday. But now, having been there (I think) and seen that it wasn't necessarily all that it's cracked up to be, what now for fans, what else can the future hold? Football fans as morbid theatre audiences; is that the future? Once you've been to the promised land, can you go back again, and will it be the same promised land?

I was not the only one reflecting on things away from the match before us. There were many here who were slightly more focussed on the day's Six Nations games, home and away fans included, with the Birmingham lot, like Wolves recently, apparently predisposed to the different shaped ball. Screens in the foyer were showing the Ireland game, and I'm fairly sure we'd have known about exciting goings on down there, with the crowd watching this game downstairs likely to make more noise than fans upstairs in the stands.

Kennedy and Doyle were brought on at half time in an attempt to liven things up. Doyle then got his goal, and it seemed like a win today was going to be a bit of a stroll in the park, with Birmingham still not offering much in response. Jones could certainly have made things easier though, if he hadn't spurned two excellent chances. Fortunately, Whitts was not going to miss from the spot, and this penalty would seal a comfortable win.

It was around this time that things turned a bit nasty in the stands. Some frustrated Birmingham fans started attacking stewards in the top corner of the away end, closest to the Family Stand. I suppose this again showed the illogic of having the Family Section right next to the away fans. But then again, does it actually make more sense to allow more 'experienced' fans next to the away section? If avoiding trouble is the key, the present set-up, though not popular, is probably the best available option, as after all, these sorts of events are very rare these days. We have not very often seen fans like this Birmingham lot wanting to cause trouble. The problem is, it's all very well to say that people shouldn't pick fights with certain types of fan; that people shouldn't pick fights with families, or those on their own, or people in replica shirts just there for the football, etc. I think if people want to pick fights, as some of the Birmingham crowd certainly looked like they wanted to, they're not going to spend too much time finding the exact matching candidates, and instead just go for whoever's nearest. In the end, it looked like one of them was even laying into the police, so no doubt he was going to face a pretty hefty sentence. Just senseless you might think.

From my vantage point, it looked as if those in the Family Section near to the away fans were not too unnerved, and seemed to deal with the situation extremely well, not allowing the away fans to rattle them, and not retaliating.

I think this was probably the most fighting I have seen in the Cardiff City Stadium, but given that it was still only a couple of skirmishes, it just goes to show how times have changed and how much less of that sort of thing is going on now. There are those who say they would like things to return to how they used to be, but is more fighting genuinely what people mean by this? Is trouble at football matches the same thing as a better atmosphere, after all, and is one needed for the other to exist? Can an atmosphere be generated without the need for potential violence?

I got the feeling this was going to be a one-off, although that's not to say that other away fans might not try a similar thing now that they'd seen Birmingham try it out, irrespective of whether they'd have also seen that those involved were obviously going to be facing bans, etc.

The walk along Sloper Road afterwards was certainly a bit more nervy than I can remember for a long time, but at least we had the satisfaction of a well earned three points.

April/May

As the decidedly lacklustre season was drawing to a close, now was the time to sort the wheat from the chaff, to sort the dedicated fan from the part-time supporter, the lunatic from someone with more common sense. There were certainly many stay-aways at the remaining few home games, and for one away fixture, it was a virtual no-show, as supporters demonstrated how we had finally had enough of treatment by the West Yorkshire police and boycotted the match against Leeds. Keeping with tradition, however, the Bluebirds still won that 2-1. Not too bad a run in, which might have been frustrating for those calling for Slade's head. If only the party spirit at the final away game against Forest might continue into the season that would lie ahead of us.

April 6
Cardiff 0-3 Bolton: Marshall Nutmegged, But Scoreline Flatters

Almost didn't make this one as was informed at Queen Street station that there were no trains, so had to make alternative plans.

The talk before this game was the rumour about a potential new manager, Bruno Ribeiro from Portugal. Given that the other talking point was the lack of season ticket sales for the next campaign, I wondered if this news was designed to spark fresh interest. My own feeling was that it might be a bit of a gamble to once again go for someone without experience. Possibly even more of a gamble than Solskjaer. Slade was not proving popular, but as he had now settled in, he could potentially provide a solid enough start to next season at least.

To put it succinctly, we were unlucky in this one. We were quite well up in the first half, with Bolton not offering all that much. In contrast to the feisty Birmingham fans, Bolton's fans won the award for quietest away fans of the season hands down; barely a murmur from them throughout the first half. Maybe they too were content to simply bask in the warm sunshine. Like us, they had nothing to play for, but you'd think even so, after travelling all this way, they would have made a bit more effort. Perhaps poor football has impacted on fans' enthusiasm – this is cited as a reason for our own librarian tendencies, but we do at least still make some noise at away games.

Given that there was absolutely nothing to play for, I did find it a shame that players, in that case, weren't playing a bit freer; maybe testing the keeper from range, taking a few more risks, the odd thirty yard volley here and there. Instead, there was still a tendency for Cardiff's players to pull up at the final fence and just not deliver. Noone got into a shooting chance not more than ten or so yards from goal, but then oddly elected to pass. For much of the season, it's seemed as if Noone has been acting strictly on instruction; there sometimes seemed little other reason for some of his more bizarre decisions. It was either strange decision making, or on other occasions, simple mistakes, and quite honestly, I would not have minded seeing Noone dropped.

Whitts on the other hand put in another solid display. You can't deny he's a good versatile player. He's very good at adapting to the players around him. The team may have chopped and changed quite a bit, but Whitts still always fitted in, adapting his passing style to suit the team that's lined up alongside him.

Malone was in again, and for the first time that I'd seen, he was given a crack at a free kick. A strange, high, looping thing which did not prove effective, but I wouldn't have minded if he was given another try.

The striker position remained one that Cardiff were having difficulty filling successfully, despite a number of options. Anyone who bemoaned the move of Jones to Bournemouth must have seriously needed their head looked at in my opinion as his contribution had been no better than any of Cardiff's other frontmen, who seemed to all redefine the meaning of the expression 'hit and miss'. They hit, and they miss. Despite what Jones had said, my take on it was that he was potentially getting a lucky free ticket back to the Premier once Bournemouth, as was looking likely, won promotion.

So anyway, this time it was Revell and Doyle, and Slade must have wondered just for how much longer he was going to have to watch yet another ineffective pairing running aimlessly around. His patience ran out before half time this time, and Joe Mason was brought on.

People had apparently been looking forward to the return of Mason. No offence to him or his supporters, but this I also found slightly bemusing. Fair enough, give the guy some backing after returning from an injury, but what major contribution did Mason ever make to the side? I wondered if for some more recent fans it was just a case of heralding the return of a player whose name they could remember! I really can't imagine there were many for whom memories of the man were of sublime finishing, or silky skills on the ball. It was fitting that he was back for this game after two loan spells at Bolton. According to his wiki page, he once got a hat-trick for them, but other than that, I can't imagine he set the world alight up there either. As far as I was concerned, he was not the miracle man people seemed to have been expecting, and no goals or even goal attempts were forthcoming from his feet.

Instead, a second half bombardment from the Wanderers ensued. Despite no real motivation from City in the first half, Bolton's passion for the game did not look any greater, so it came as a bit of a surprise when they suddenly stepped up a gear or two. Marshall was easily beaten three times, getting nutmegged for the second, and you had to wonder where Bolton had suddenly found the energy from. City did not have the excuse that they only had one day to prepare since their last game on Saturday – Bolton were in the same boat, having played on Saturday also, unlike many Championship teams who would not have played since Good Friday.

Marshall recovered to make a good save and prevent a fourth goal, but in terms of a fightback, Cardiff weren't able to offer all that much. But that's not to say they were well beaten in this game. I thought they once again played ok, a few iffy passes aside, and were not easily beaten; the scoreline definitely flattered Bolton.

The goals woke the Bolton fans up, and we got to hear their rendition of the English national anthem, to which Dai Hunt, a couple of rows in front of me, replied with a shout of Sieg Heil, which got a few laughs. I was thinking of starting the occasional feature of 'great Dai Hunt one man chants' on the blog. The feature would basically be dedicated to things Dai Hunt shouts out, to which nobody ever responds, except perhaps for a few titters of laughter. It could be extended to include other one man chants (might even include my own in these); let's face it, one man chants are becoming increasingly common with many in the crowd too lazy to bother joining in. Anyone with any suggestions for inclusions to this feature, are invited to send them in using the hashtag, onemanwenttomow.

With around five minutes to go, and with City showing no great urgency, I did see something that I did think was touching. Fabio was waiting for the ball to be returned to him by a young ballboy, or maybe someone in one of the front rows. With five minutes remaining on the clock, under normal circumstances, you might hope he would urge the hasty return of the ball with the hope of getting a goal, but instead, he waited patiently, and you know what, I didn't mind. He displayed a certain professional spirit, I thought, in being patient despite the circumstances. I think he is generally a good advert for the game, and we're lucky to have a player like him in our team.

So of course, the game ended, and up went the Slade Out chants, despite this being just our third defeat in thirteen, and I honestly didn't think we played that badly, and definitely didn't deserve to lose by three. They say you can't make an omelette without breaking eggs, but making an omelette without any eggs at all is an even harder task.

April 9
Dannie Abse: A Cardiff City Fanatic

There are three types of 'celebrity' football fans. The first of these are the players and ex-players, who of course have an affiliation through some club or other, though not always the club they were most well known for playing at; it might be the team they grew up supporting, but whichever it is, obviously this type of celebrity fan is easy to understand. Gathered into this group are all the football pundits, who are usually ex-players, though not always, but anyway, as I say, this is the easy to understand, regular celebrity football fan.

The next type is your Frank Skinner. This is a celebrity, maybe a comedian, or a TV presenter, or a TV presenter who fancies himself as a comedian. One of those sorts of people. Angus Deayton. That sort. These are the people famous for being known to support a team. They're so well known for supporting the team – because they're always fecking banging on about it – that their name and the name of the football club are often regularly mentioned in the same sentence. Publicity-wise for both club and celeb, it probably works quite well. For the ordinary fan of the club, it might get a bit grating at times. Unless you're a fan of both the club and the celeb. Perhaps a lot of fans of the club become fans of the celeb because they're fans of the club. Unless it's David Mellor.

Finally, there's the worst type of course. These are the ones that suddenly appear 'as if by magic' when a team is suddenly enjoying its time in the sun. When a team is suddenly doing well, fans the club never knew they had suddenly pop up from nowhere and are seen hob-nobbing with the chairman. And if the team suddenly falls from grace, mysteriously, this type of fan seems to fade into the background as well. How can this be? It's almost as if this type of fan manufactured the club's brief period of success themselves, because as quickly as the club drops down a league, the celebrity fan is no longer seen at games – surely not a complete coincidence?

Well, Cardiff City does not have any major league celebrity fans. We certainly don't have an Elton John. Maybe it's partly because we're not a major league team. Of course, we've got a smattering of semi-famous celebrity ex-players, but we're never going to have too many of those, because we haven't spawned too many famous players to enable the coming about of famous celebrity ex-players. We have Neil Kinnock, although I'm not sure if anyone knows quite what category he falls into. In some ways, he's a bit of a famous failure, but he is definitely famous, as Maggie Thatcher's main rival. But nobody seems to know exactly when he started supporting Cardiff City. He was there in the Sam Hammam era, but I'm not sure if anyone knows if he was there before that. So he could fall into the category of famous failure who was there when we were doing pretty well (though not phenomenally well, still nowhere near the Premiership). And while I don't think he's actually jumped ship just yet, he hasn't been seen doing quite so much hob-nobbing as he once did.

Probably Cardiff City's most famous fans are actually people who are basically famous for being Cardiff City fans, like Tony Rivers and Annis Abraham, which is interesting, and perhaps says something about the club, though I'm not sure what exactly. Both have popular books available.

Dannie Abse was someone who was hardly a celebrity, but

well known and well respected in the fairly limited field of poetry, and known, but not well known, as being a Cardiff City fan. However, in fairness to Dannie Abse, whether he was well known or not as a person, or as a fan, probably mattered absolutely diddly squat to him. This was a man, I have learned from reading his own article published in the excellent *The Great Crowd Roars* (Parthian), who was completely obsessed with Cardiff City throughout his whole life. Maybe not a lot of people realise that.

In this article, Dannie tells of how he planned his poetry readings around the country to coincide with Cardiff City away games. Very clever thinking, I thought. No wonder he was also a doctor! But that's not the main point. The main point is that in this article, Dannie uses the language of the uber-fan. He talks about having dreams about Cardiff City. He talks about things like having the *Echo* sent over to him while he was abroad. Hats off to him, he clearly was an uber-fan.

I used to occasionally see him when going to games at Ninian Park. I was just starting to learn about the Cardiff poetry scene, and I knew he was considered to be a pretty major player, but I didn't know him any more than to maybe say hello to and acknowledge him. I did occasionally get into a short conversation with him. This would have been at the time I was selling programmes in the 99/00 season most likely. What I do recall is that he would only ever want to talk about Cardiff City. Despite his status, Dannie Abse was absolutely a Cardiff City fan, with the same hopes and fears as the rest of us.

I remember once going to see Dannie read some poetry in Waterstones. In fact, I even mentioned the occasion in a poem I wrote called 'Sad'. I would go on to write four more in the 'Sad' series of poems, but Dannie is only mentioned in the first one which goes as follows:

Sad

Stock Aitken & Waterman saved Brother Beyond,
But I bet they never believed,
Eight years after its release,
Someone would buy their live video
From a discount bookshop in Cardiff.

With time on my hands, I'd gone in to see
If they still stocked Jeff Koons postcards
Like they did a couple of years ago.
Inevitably, I glanced at the music section,
And there it was behind a Ned's Atomic Dustbin video.

I didn't buy it immediately.
I first went to an amusement arcade
And threw away the money I could have spent
Buying the video into a Big Breakfast machine,
Never once getting the feature.

Then I went to see Dannie Abse
Read some poetry in Waterstone's.
While I watched him, I planned my purchase.
Dannie is, by his own admission, out of date.
He could never reminisce about the tragedy that was Brother Beyond.

Well, then I went with Spide to get some money out
And made one of the saddest purchases ever made
Just before the shop shut.
Back home, I watched Nathan strut his stuff
And the ugly ones being ugly, all in dreadful t-shirts. I revelled in sadness.

I think there may well have been something like an almost twenty year gap between that reading and the next time I went to see him read, which was at a First Thursday event, organised by his publisher, Seren Books, at Chapter just a few years ago (around 2011). I had just recently befriended a woman, who I shall refer to as K, who I would, perhaps unwisely, continue to be involved with for another couple of years. Anyway, it had been a month since we'd first met at a party I'd arranged. She lived in the Valleys, and I'd arranged to meet her off the train before going on to Chapter.

Sadly, when I met her at the station she was extremely drunk – practically falling on the floor drunk at around eight in the evening. I managed to get her in the car, and then made the grave decision of still taking her to the poetry event, mainly because I was keen to go myself, but partly also because this had been the plan, and I've always liked sticking to plans, no matter what, and also, there was no alternative plan (I'm sure I could have hastily thought one up, but still).

We arrived late at the poetry reading, and made quite a noisy entrance. In her drunken state, K proceeded to talk quite loudly to me, and when she couldn't hear my whispered replies she would keep saying 'What? WHAT??!' and then she kept saying, very loudly, she didn't want to be there etc. No amount of shushing would keep her quiet, and everyone around us was getting noticeably upset by it all. I was just embarrassed of course. What I didn't realise was that the event was being filmed and K had effectively ruined the whole filming. I think it was going to be one of the few chances they were going to get to film Dannie in a live setting.

Nonetheless, I could not have quite anticipated what happened next. As the session was closing a man of large ego and apparently low social skills bounded up to K and well...

we were manhandled to the door in the apparent drunken chaos of a Dannie Abse poetry reading by a self-appointed bouncer.

We were assisted on the evening by Simon Hicks of Seren Books, who was very sympathetic in the circumstances. We had just ruined his night but he was polite and calm and seemed to show some understanding of K's condition.

I didn't speak to Dannie Abse on that night but I sent him a letter of apology, which he acknowledged, along with a letter to Simon Hicks of Seren, who also acknowledged my letter, and one of complaint to 'the bouncer', who I do not recall replied at all.

Maybe I should never have been involved with K in the first place, and should probably have not maintained my friendship for as long as I did, but the actions of this other person were almost unforgiveable. K had been so drunk that she forgot the incident completely. This was sadly often the case when she got drunk.

My next reading engagement that involved Dannie Abse was at a function organised to commemorate Dannie's life as a City fan, to take place next to the Cardiff City Stadium. Dannie had passed away in the autumn of 2014. I had an email from Professor Tony Curtis giving details about this event. I contacted Professor Curtis asking if I could read a poem at this event and received the very curt reply (pun intended) that the schedule was full up, but I took a couple of poems along nonetheless, and hopped on the train from Queen Street to Ninian Park station (I had recently relinquished my driving licence) in time for the function at 12.30pm.

Mike Jenkins, of the Red Poets in Merthyr, who was actually the chief organiser of the event, bounded up to me and immediately asked if I could read a poem. Now I realise that Curtis might not actually know me, and might not have known that I was a fellow City fan, along with Mike, but I did find the whole situation typically amusing. Julie Pritchard, who had been doing a sterling job of keeping the Rhyme and Real Ale night going, was also there, and was also asked by Mike to read a poem.

So the short ceremony (hardly a long, jam packed schedule that could not be altered) got underway, and Curtis said a few words, and in fact, I did think he spoke well. Mike read one of Dannie's poems; Cary Archard, who was my old English teacher at school, who was speaking in his capacity as friend and publisher of Dannie, also spoke, before Julie and I read our poems. I read the following one about the end of the last season at Ninian Park, which went down quite well, I think:

Missed Out

I applauded the last, and the away team's third,
At the last ever game at Ninian Park;
We missed out on the play-offs, have you heard?

The manner in which it happened was quite absurd,
The extent of the collapse was clearly stark,
We ended up seventh, when we could have been third.

On the last day, it was as many had feared,
Cardiff failed to make their mark,
Pipped by Preston, seemed totally weird.

Three games before, a 6-0 loss was incurred,
The players, it would seem, had lost their spark,
And suddenly everything was kind of blurred.

But still, not to make it seemed absurd,
A draw with Charlton, before back to Nin Park,
And hope that the players had now been spurred.

But when Ipswich knocked in the last, and their third,
Suddenly the world seemed incredibly dark,
This was just surreal, how could it have occurred?

No longer feel like being a Bluebird,
Especially with the closing of Ninian Park,
If it hadn't been for the away team's third,
We'd have made the play-offs, haven't you heard?

Then it was just left for the plaque to be placed beneath the designated tree, near to the old Ninian Park gates for Dannie, and the brief but quite touching occasion was finished. People were invited to nearby Chapter Arts, and as I was not driving, Julie kindly gave me a lift over.

Here, I met Dannie's daughter, Keren, who was very nice, and I signed a copy of my book for her which included the poem I read. I also met a couple of media characters, including the guy who does the commentary for Cardiff City's website, and for the Cardiff City DVDs. A funny old guy, I've always thought his to be a fairly old fashioned style of commentary, and he definitely had the look of someone who'd come from the old school, but nice enough. I wasn't quite sure who his friend was, but he had a very similar sounding voice to the Radio Wales cricket commentator, Edward Bevan, though he did assure me it wasn't he. It's always funny putting a face to someone you know better for their voice, although in this latter case, it was the wrong face! The two of them, Richard Shepherd (the Cardiff commentator) and the guy who wasn't Edward Bevan, were a right couple of stattos, to be honest – they probably could have not only named the scorers for Cardiff on the day Dannie Abse was born, but also, who was booked, the number of corners, and probably even who the ref was on the day!

Well, anyway, a nice occasion, I finally shuffled off, and I did afterwards get an email from Tony Curtis. It read, simply, in that familiar curt style: 'Thank you for your contribution to today's event [*which I was not the organiser of*]. You are clearly a serious fan.' He did not get a further reply.

April 18
Church Mice 0-0 Tame Lions

Not sure if I could have projected a softer image walking towards Kiwi's. The coffee shop next door was giving out free mini frappuccinos, which I was unable to resist, so I was walking towards this large group of lads outside Kiwi's with what looked like an ice cream in one hand, and a mobile phone to my ear in the other, and with a rucksack (to be explained) on my back, and as I did so, at the last minute, I sort of skirted round the outside of the assembled crowd, suddenly not certain if these were Cardiff or Millwall fans.

What is it about this fixture that inspires large numbers of lads in Cardiff to go into town dressed in smart designer clothes and stand around outside pubs? I'd decided I would walk in to see if anything was going on, God knows why, maybe I was reminded of the opening game of the season in '99, when a large number of Millwall fans had been put into the pub on the corner of Mill Lane. On that occasion, I'd also been in town, and had actually walked through a line of police towards these fans, thinking that they were Cardiff fans, before quite quickly realising my error and backtracking.

Not sure why I'd have imagined this time that it wouldn't be Cardiff fans in Kiwi's – not a likely venue for away fans as one of Cardiff's most traditional of venues – and when I recognised a couple of faces, I was reassured. But with friends now sick of consistently poor home performances not even bothering with this one I was on my own, and suddenly not quite sure what to do with myself. It was about 2.30, so too late to order a pint, I thought, if I was going to make the match.

It was pretty apparent to me that there were a large number of these fans who didn't really have much interest in going to the game at all, as with time ticking on and the ground a half hour walk away, there were no signs of readiness being made to leave. They were probably people who had not actually attended a game of football for years, preferring the sport of standing around outside a pub looking hard.

I did see a few groups of Millwall fans milling around town, shouting and looking quite dangerous. They really do not seem to have a care in the world, Millwall fans. They are quite unlike most fans who will at least make some effort to not be quite so blatant about their identity as they stroll round the town of the opposing team.

So anyway, I stood around for probably not more than about a minute, wondering if anything was going to happen, but it did occur to me that probably all that was going to happen was that people would just continue standing around indefinitely. For blogging purposes, I wondered whether it would be better if I stayed to see if anything other than just standing around would transpire, but instead, I headed for my intended destination, the train station, only to be told that the train to Ninian Park was cancelled, surprise, surprise. But from Cardiff Central, it's not too far a walk to the ground. I got chatting to a guy from Ebbw Vale whose mates were also not bothering with this one.

It seemed like most people had friends who'd started just not bothering to come to games, despite having season tickets, and most people had friends who were talking about not renewing next season. It had become a bit depressing really. Surely a team is entitled to one duff season, you'd think, but it seemed like it was about more than just that.

People were just not happy about the match day experience in general, and I could have warned that this might have happened years ago. Under Malky Mackay in the Championship, for example, it could sometimes still be deathly silent, and then with some slightly lacklustre football, we might get one goal, and a win, and fortunately, we were still having moderate success, so people still came back. Take away those few goals, and take away a few of those wins, we would not have been vying for promotion and it would have been the same scenario, except that at least at that time there was the added incentive for some fans of renewing early, with a structure that meant cheaper tickets for these fans. With that system having effectively expired, there was now less of an incentive. For sure, a good number of people would still be renewing, albeit with a degree of reluctance, at some point over the close season, but without doubt, in general, things were not good.

But back to the matter in hand – this particular match. The Millwall fans looked a little cramped, squeezed into a smallish part of the away section. There were not all that many of them, but I'm not sure if this was to do with them having a limited allocation. Otherwise, you might have thought that a team in the midst of a relegation battle (which they were far more likely to be on the worse side of if they lost this game) would have a larger contingency of supporters, but then again, maybe some of the Millwall lot also preferred the sport of hanging around outside a pub looking hard, and were not bothering to attend the match itself, despite having travelled all this way.

In terms of the standard of the football this was one of the worst games of the season with both teams to blame. The away team, in the second half, the main culprits, with some pretty dire missed chances. There was a good case for standing around outside a pub being a better option as a way of spending the afternoon, rather than watching this rubbish. Even the referee had a poor game, so there was not one person on the pitch who put in a performance of merit.

About twenty minutes into the match, I'm sure I saw a couple of people who had been standing around outside Kiwi's take their places in the Ninian Stand, so maybe standing around outside the pub had not proved to be a much more entertaining past-time after all. I learned from someone during my customary half-time fag break that a number of fans had also been seen standing around along Sloper Road during the first half.

But back to the match again, and it was the Family Stand that enjoyed the best view of the lions' share of the action, with most of the chances being directed at the goal in front of them. For Cardiff in the first half, Doyle had a reasonable effort saved, before Whitts took a punt from range, and I wondered if he'd read my last report suggesting that the team might as well try some more speculative shots, with nothing much to lose.

Towards the end of the first half, a looping shot from Ralls hit the bar; near to the start of the second half, it was a Millwall player, with a shot that took everyone by surprise, hitting the same cross bar. There then followed a couple of parodic pieces of play from Millwall which involved them getting into the box and then more-or-less just falling over the ball. Really not much for the Lions to roar about, but they didn't need to be loud to show up the Bluebirds in our alter egos as church mice.

Millwall's fate, and whether or not they could retain their status in this league, now rested on whether Rotherham, one place above them, would have points deducted for fielding an illegible player. Cardiff's fate, in terms of its fan basis, seemed a lot more uncertain, despite our Championship place already being booked.

It was just lucky for me that I had something afterwards to focus my attention on. My girlfriend was playing in a poker tournament in Nottingham and I hopped on a train (see earlier reference to backpack) to go and meet her. This proved to be an altogether more successful outing, but that's a whole other story...

April 25
Cardiff 3-2 Blackpool: Kids' Cheers Lift Lid of Upper Tier

As the team that scuppered our chances in the play-off final in 2010, I suppose I've felt a bit of resentment towards Blackpool ever since. It had to be someone I suppose. But I never liked their then manager Ian Holloway either, with his cheeky chappy ways and his annoying Bristolian accent (my second least favourite accent after the Birmingham accent). On reflection, I think we were a lot better prepared for the Premier that time. We had a good solid team. We had the likes of Joe Ledley, Bothroyd, Chopra, a Whitts on form, and Bellamy would surely have still joined us the following season. You could argue that after all his effort, maybe Dave Jones did deserve to have been the manager that took us up. For many fans, if we'd gone up that season, it would have meant having their season tickets refunded as a reward, and that would have surely escalated fans' fervour even further. We would have gone up in blue!

And let's face it, we were unlucky in that game, against a

Blackpool side who didn't seem especially good, and then proved it in their single season in the Premier League. With the team we had at that time, we would have stood a far greater chance of survival, I expect. So when it came to this fixture, I was just a little reticent about joining in with the cheers and boos for Blackpool and their mutual bad situationism with regard to being opposed to modern football. I read a good article about all the terrible things their owner, Owen Oyston, has done, and you can understand fans' frustration. But still, isn't that their problem? For how much longer are we going to have to pursue this line of always having to stick up for fans who, like us, have had it stuck to them a bit?

That's not to say I didn't very much dislike seeing Blackpool fans getting ejected for holding up banners of opposition. But then that feeling came not so much from being on the side of the Blackpool fans, but from being opposed to our stewards and the fact that they felt the need once again to be excessively heavy handed, just as they have with our own fans. With numbers dwindling, to see anyone being made to leave without an overwhelming due cause is a bit alarming.

With Blackpool already relegated, and with us already cemented in a mid-table position, it might have been the case that there was nothing riding on this game, but as Blackpool had not won a single game on their travels all season, this of course meant that they might at least have a strong desire to chalk up their one and only away win, and at the same time, it would be nice for us to try our darndest not to allow this to happen and save us the embarrassment. We after all had a pretty poor record against teams at the foot of the table this season, both home and away.

Any jitters Cardiff may have felt were eased on the thirtieth minute when Mason slotted in the opening goal, and it was chill pills all round when we won a penalty which Doyle struck home making it 2-0 at the break. Half time fags were a lot less stressful, for fans at least, not sure about in the players' dressing room.

I could hardly stop myself applauding, in a semi-sympathetic way, when Blackpool got one back after the break, but another Doyle penalty, making it 3-1 to Cardiff, meant that surely the absolute best Blackpool could hope for now would be a draw? They did get one more back, but the scoreline would remain at 3-2, and in many ways it was relief all round, probably for both sets of fans. 'Thank God that's over!' was the headline of Cardiff City blog, the Mauve and Yellow Army, with all our home fixtures completed, and with a troublesome campaign drawing to a close.

For Blackpool fans, who, along with holding up banners of protest, also had comical banners, including one stating 'Campaign Conference: Stage 1 Complete', clearly, it was a case of not knowing whether to laugh or cry, as they even did the conga at one stage. There must have been fans who had made every away game of the season who were absolutely pulling their hair out.

My publisher came along to this one, and he really enjoyed it. In fairness, it wasn't a bad game; the goal tally helped, of course, but actually, he surprised me and said it was the atmosphere that he enjoyed most! I've grown tired of having to apologise to people about how it's not like it was at Ninian Park, etc. I think he was able to get caught up in the occasion though, and it made a change from having to hear constant moaners, never happy with the way things are. There was after all some interaction with the away fans for this game; if anything, the loudest noise from Cardiff fans was in support of Blackpool's situation.

There was one thing my publisher said that I thought was very telling. He said it does seem that when things go right, everyone has a great time, and it's all good, but if things don't go well, there's the finger pointing and finding people to blame, instead of just accepting that that's the way things go sometimes... I don't know, maybe that's not quite right – there are clubs, like Man Utd, where there's been success, but fans have still had a go at the owners. And even Cardiff of course – we were getting promoted to the Premier League, but people were booing Tan! I do wonder in Blackpool's case though – if they weren't getting relegated, would there be the same attacks on the owner? Perhaps there would have been, but should fans perhaps consider sitting back and being fans who cheer and support the team rather than forever worrying themselves with backroom goings on, and being almost too involved with the football club?

There was the usual laughter when the attendance figures were announced, as yet again, numbers looked down, meaning that non-attending season ticket holders must again have been included in the figures (surely this has to stop?). However, one initiative for this game was to allow kids in for free in the new tier above the Ninian Stand. I think it must have been almost filled up, and this itself helped with the atmosphere a little – there was certainly more of a background hum throughout the whole match, and during exciting moments of play, it was nice to hear some additional soprano vocals added to the more usual bass tones. There was a slightly comic moment when a linesman flagged for offside, the kids obviously didn't realise, and still cheered when the ball went in the net – suddenly, there was a whole lot of noise coming from just one part of the ground! They would have to brush up on their football knowledge, these youngsters, if they were going to start coming down regularly, which must have been the hope.

The question of who else would still be coming down regularly would remain an issue. There seemed to be enough people who were continuing to say they'd support the team no matter what, but there were also plenty of people saying they'd had enough. It might be hard to pinpoint exactly what the meaning of having had enough in this context meant, but my own view was that the club needed to work on doing things that would keep fans coming back. Single game initiatives are good, like letting the kids in free for this match, or encouraging people to wear old replica shirts. But also, there were things that could be done to improve things throughout the season – look at pricing, look at the range of beer available, look at having a more relaxed approach from stewards, basically positive steps instead of strict control. Long term, you'd think bringing in safe standing would have to be the key, but then again, if it is just a better atmosphere that's needed, just about every set of away fans at the Cardiff City Stadium has proved that atmosphere can be generated at this ground (even if it may be true that most of these fans are standing), but also, the atmosphere at Wales games at the CCS is always good, and just look at how much better the atmosphere was in our first game back in blue. We can do it, we just need more of a push; constantly blaming the club and the team is not going to help, we as fans need to also look at ourselves and question why we have become so lazy as supporters!

May 2
Nottingham Forest 1-2 Cardiff City: 'We're mid-table more than you!'

Last game of the season heralds hordes in fancy dress: I spotted the Jamaican Bob Sleigh team, a couple of Where's Wallies, the odd bloke as a banana, and no end of nuns. One guy on the bus I travelled up with joked that there were also going to be eleven men dressed as footballers, meaning the Cardiff City team!

In fairness, the conclusion of the season was not so bad, with just two defeats in the last ten, and more wins than draws. Our away form was particularly good – a victory against Forest would make it three away wins in five, with just the one loss. Again, someone said, not entirely in jest, that a win in this game would not be such a good thing as it would probably guarantee that Slade would hang on to his job.

It was a dilemma, there was no doubt about that. Slade had hardly endeared himself to fans, but his record on paper was not all that bad, despite some decidedly iffy performances. He had steadied the ship after Solskjaer's severe rocking of said boat. But had he put it on course for an altogether better journey? With the election looming, his own claims could be compared to those of the Tories who said that they had steadied the economy after Labour's over-spending. Don't change course now was the Conservatives' warning, and Cardiff had a similar quandry. Did Slade actually deserve to be sacked, despite his unpopularity? As opposed to the British public's relatively straightforward option of simply going back to Labour, Cardiff would have a much wider range of options in terms of possible managers that could be brought in – Warburton from Brentford had been mentioned, and there were surely many others – but could any of these guarantee better things? Unless there was a manager who could be set in stone certain as a better prospect from the word go, was it not worth seeing if Slade could at least get us off to a good start? But then, I suppose that was the thinking behind keeping on Solksjaer at the start of this last campaign, and the poor start he had meant it was always going to be difficult for the Bluebirds to achieve much in the 2014/15 season, whoever was brought in. Did we really want the same thing happening, ie. give Slade a similar chance, only to see by October that he had to go?

If there was one positive about next season to reflect on, it would of course be that we would be starting the season in blue, so fans at least did not have that to worry about. And the return to blue was after all put in place under Slade's reign. People do not give him credit for this – it may well be the case that Slade himself was hardly influential in this matter, but it was something, when he took over, that he expressed concern about. For this reason alone, I'm not sure it's right to cast Slade as another of Tan's yes-men; surely Mackay could have said something about changing the club's colours – his regret at not doing this may have been partially a reason for his falling out with Tan – and then there was Solskjaer who probably felt that affecting a rebrand reversal was the least of his concerns.

If there was not much riding on City's last home game against Blackpool, there was even less to make this a meaningful fixture, with both teams going into it smack bang in the middle of the table, level on points, with even the same stats in terms of overall wins, draws and defeats. I suppose this did at least mean that the winner of this tie would finish higher in the table than the other. Bearing in mind Cardiff's recent form, I felt 11/4 were pretty generous odds, and had a couple of quid on just a Cardiff victory. I had to wait around for the guy manning the bookies in the ground to even show up – there was clearly not a feeling of being desperate to take money from anyone who'd travelled from South Wales. I also put a couple of small bets on Noone to score. I literally ran into him in the St David's shopping arcade in the week leading up to this fixture – he was running, I think, to get back to his car (perhaps even footballers worry about car parking prices?!), but he at least had time to stop to shake my hand. I didn't ask for a photo or for his autograph – apart from the fact that he was clearly in a rush, it might have been slightly embarrassing after, in a previous report, I had suggested he could be dropped! It's always nice to meet City players unexpectedly though, whether they are the current flavour of the month or not.

The Notts Forest bookies had a special, offering 600/1 for a Noone/4-0, which might have sounded a bit absurd, but again, I couldn't resist. It was immediately apparent once the game kicked off that the likelihood of this happening was even less than might have been imagined as Noone was not after all given a start. At least this meant I'd be getting money back on the bets I'd placed on him just to score. Whitts was also not in the team, so whether it was due to injuries or not, the two players whose form people had been questioning were not going to have the opportunity of changing people's opinions of them. Could their absence even mean an improved overall performance?

I think it would be difficult to argue this case in a nothing game such as this one, particularly as the Forest team appeared to show an almost complete lack of interest in it themselves. This really was one of the easiest games we'd had all season, and you just wished we could have had a few more of these. As opposed to City fans, who were on some kind of mission to enjoy themselves at least, the home crowd were completely non-plussed. I recall the volume of the home support here at the City Ground to be amongst the best I've ever heard, but by complete contrast, today they were silent almost throughout the game. Coupled with poor season fatigue, large sections of 'sterile areas' between sets of fans, just as we now have at the CCS, were probably largely to blame – very sad, in my view, that officials are enforcing these atmosphere-killing methods.

It seems like there are just so many things in force at the moment to hinder fans' enjoyment – from enforced seating, to brutal segregation, from pricing policies to strict rules about smoking. At so many grounds these days, with no options available (many grounds do not allow fans to leave the stadium), fans are forced to have their half-time cigarettes in toilets – not enjoyable, and technically against the law – it's hardly an ideal solution.

I can't say I was really concentrating on on-field matters too much for this one. What I do know is that in less than half an hour, Cardiff had made concentrating less of a concern, by granting fans a 2-0 lead. Ralls got the first following a well-worked sequence of passes; Doyle doubled the lead soon after – increasingly Doyle was looking like someone who might finally be the effective frontman we have sought for some considerable time now. With the team cruising, enjoyment of the occasion became a lot easier – I started to wonder if we might go on to get one of those freak results and a glut of goals, but though Forest were still not offering much, they were just about keeping us at bay, at least.

The main chant we sing at Forest of course centres around referring to them as 'scabs'. From a personal point of view, I am less inclined to sing this one after meeting a former miner from Nottingham at a Stone Roses fans' convention last year. From what this guy told me, he had been no scab, and gave the impression that the term was really not appropriate for many of the miners from the region at that time. I suppose just as we've learned to put up with the term sheep-shaggers, Forest fans can probably live with scab as a term of abuse, but I suppose the difference is, the term scab could be considered personal and based on some kind of reality, whereas the term sheep-shagger of course has no basis whatsoever when it comes to reality. None whatsoever.

Today, fans decided to really go to town with songs for Wales as well. If Cardiff City were not quite generating the excitement they might, it was good that fans of the Welsh national side had something to look forward to, with the prospect of a trip to France looking like a dead cert.

The only thing that marred this occasion in terms of it being one for fans to savour was the sending off of Marshall towards the end. What we knew that Forest might not have done however was that Moore had proved himself an able replacement, and he was quickly called into action, with a good piece of goalkeeping very soon after Marshall's dismissal. Forest did get the one goal back, but there was no time for an equaliser, and so the win, and a respectable enough 11th place finish for City, was sealed.

There were a whole host of reasons for City fans to not be over the moon about things as we went into the holiday period, but to some extent, cares could be cast aside at this last game of the season. Whereas after our last home game, there was a sense of relief that it was all over, after this final game, there was more of a sense that maybe, just maybe, we might now have something to look forward to next season.

And so that was it for Cardiff for another year. Unlike some fans who, even in the close season, seem to like to still get constant updates with regard to the club, transfer rumours, etc, for me, it's a time to relax and follow other pursuits without the stress of worrying about football – so long as it's not a year ending in an even number of course, when there will still be either the World Cup or the Euros.

This year though, there was one game in the close season that, it seemed, every Welshman and his wife was looking forward to, and that was Wales' qualifying game against Belgium. After doing so well in other group matches, interest in this one was frenzied, and it sold out before a lot of fans, including myself, even had time to think about getting tickets. It was annoying – I know plenty of people who missed out, many of whom were long-standing Welsh football fans who had just not got round to getting a ticket.

But no matter, I watched it in a pub – the Queen's Vaults to be precise. Wales were now ranked 22nd in the World, their highest ever placing; Belgium, inexplicably, despite not having won a single tournament, or even getting to a semi-final, were ranked 2nd! Personally, I was sure this was a bit of an anomaly, and had a good feeling that Wales, despite being better than 3/1 at the bookies, actually had a good chance of winning.

And so it came to pass that when the legend that is Gareth Bale knocked in the only goal of the match, I found myself standing on my chair, raising a glass in celebration. Christina would be joining me soon after finishing work, and at her request, I'd put a bet on Bale, so I knew she'd be happy. Here I was, standing on a chair, cheering in the middle of a pub in town, wearing RED, funnily enough. But that's the way it's always been. Wales have always been red, and always will be. Cardiff City? We'll always be BLUE!!